Earth Spirit Dream

"This precious book will help you rediscover, (first time, your vital connection to our endangered, though still enchanted, Earth. Inspired by traditional wisdom, leading-edge science, and ecosophical thought, the simple but profound exercises lead one out of the spiritual wasteland of the industrial growth society and into an experience of the deeper ecological self, a self as ancient as the seasons and rooted in the nourishing cycles of life."

— SEAN KELLY, Ph.D., philosopher, professor, and author of
Coming Home: The Birth and Transformation of the Planetary Era

"It's almost cliché to realize that reconnecting to the Earth is of paramount importance if humanity—or some significant portion thereof—is to survive and thrive into the next century. But an intellectual realization is only a first step. We need to practice having an ongoing *felt sense* of this connection. Elizabeth Meacham offers a dazzling, just-in-the-nick-of-time collection of practices to do just that."

— BILL PFEIFFER, deep ecologist, teacher, shamanic guide, founder and director
of the Sacred Earth Network, and author of *Wild Earth, Wild Soul*

"As climate catastrophe forces us to confront a world dangerously out of balance, there is a vital need to reconnect with the deep wisdom of the Earth. Our common home is not a resource to be exploited but a living magical being who needs our love and attention. Elizabeth Meacham returns us to our shamanic heritage, awakening us to our embodied spiritual intelligence. With simple but powerful practices she shows how to bring light and healing to our suffering planet and become co-creators of a new dream for humanity and the Earth. *Earth Spirit Dreaming* offers valuable tools to re-vision a world both whole and holy, a gateway to the love and joy and truth to be found as we become more firmly rooted in the Earth."

— LLEWELLYN VAUGHAN-LEE, Ph.D., teacher, author, Sufi mystic,
and editor of *Spiritual Ecology: The Cry of the Earth*

Earth Spirit Dreaming

SHAMANIC ECOTHERAPY PRACTICES

Elizabeth E. Meacham, Ph.D.

FINDHORN PRESS

Findhorn Press
One Park Street
Rochester, Vermont 05767
www.findhornpress.com

SUSTAINABLE FORESTRY INITIATIVE Certified Sourcing
www.sfiprogram.org
SFI-00854

Text stock is SFI certified

Findhorn Press is a division of Inner Traditions International

Copyright © 2020 by Elizabeth E. Meacham, Ph.D.

All rights reserved. No part of this book may be reproduced or utilized in any form or by any means, electronic or mechanical, including photocopying, recording, or by any information storage and retrieval system, without permission in writing from the publisher.

Disclaimer
The information in this book is given in good faith and is neither intended to diagnose any physical or mental condition nor to serve as a substitute for informed medical advice or care. The author of this book does not dispense medical advice nor prescribe the use of any technique as a form of treatment for medical problems. Please contact your health professional for medical advice and treatment. Neither author nor publisher can be held liable by any person for any loss or damage whatsoever which may arise directly or indirectly from the use of this book or any of the information therein.

A CIP record for this title is available from the Library of Congress

ISBN 978-1-62055-987-1 (print)
ISBN 978-1-62055-988-8 (ebook)

Printed and bound in the United States by Lake Book Manufacturing, Inc. The text stock is SFI certified. The Sustainable Forestry Initiative® program promotes sustainable forest management.

10 9 8 7 6 5 4 3 2 1

Edited by Jacqui Lewis
Text design and layout by Damian Keenan
Symbol illustrations by Elenshine, Dreamstime.com
This book was typeset in Calluna and Calluna Sans
with Bebas Neue Pro used as a display typeface.

To send correspondence to the author of this book, mail a first-class letter to the author c/o Inner Traditions • Bear & Company, One Park Street, Rochester, VT 05767, USA, and we will forward the communication, or contact the author directly at **www.elizabethmeacham.com**

For my husband, Mattuck

Let the rivers run

Contents

Foreword by Christopher M. Bache 11

Part 1: Introduction 13

1. Introduction: Waking Up to Earth 15
   From Earth-Connection to Earth-Care 16
   Slowing Down 19
   Earth Spirit Dreaming: Three Steps for
       Re-Visioning Our Planetary Stories 21

2. How to Use This Book: Growing the Gifts
   of Ecological Consciousness 29
   Working with This book 30
   Daily Practice of Rituals 32
   A Method for Discovering Magic 33
   Prepare, Prepare, Prepare 35
   Coming Home 36

3. Everything Is Connected: A Brief Introduction to Visionary
   Environmental Thought 39
   A Shifting Sense of Self: From Separation
       to Care and Connection 40
   The Participatory Worldview 43
   From Environmental Theory to Earth-Connecting Practices 50

Part 2: Earth-Connecting Practices 53

4. Earth-Connecting: The First Step of Earth Spirit Dreaming 55
   Transforming Sustenance 55
   Developing Earth-Connected Consciousness 58

5. Coming to Our Senses: Slowing Down, Tuning In, Waking Up 66
   Doing Nothing 67
   Cultivating Boredom 67

6. Cultivating Ecomindfulness: Increasing Our
   Conscious Connection with Nature 71
   Ecomindfulness Practices 73

7. Returning to the Land: Connecting with the Rhythms
   and Cycles of Nature 84
   My Special Place: The Chagrin River 91

8. Nature Art Rituals: Earth-Connecting through Creativity 93
   Nature Art Rituals in Sacred Places 94

Part 3: Spirit-Connecting Practices 103

9. Spirit-Connecting: Working with Light and Vibrational Reality 105
   Portals to Guides in Vibrational Reality 107
   Incorporating Revelation into the "Everyday" 110
   Raising Vibrations: A Full-Time Job 112

10. Sacred Space and Preparation for Working with Light 117
    How to Know Vibrational Reality 118

11. Opening to Vibrational Reality 127

12. Karmic Eddies: Personal Vibrational Healing 137

Part 4: Dream-Connecting Practices 145

13. Dream-Connecting: Creating New Stories in Vibrational Reality 147
    Dreaming as Co-Creation 148
    Vibrational Experience in Western Cultures 150
    Magic, Imagination, and the Quantum Self 155
    River Light 157

14. Sacred Rituals: Pathways to Re-Dreaming the World 159
    Western Earth-Honoring Sacraments 162
    Creating Rituals for Earth Spirit Dreaming 165

15.	Dreaming with Mandalas: Journeying with Sacred Circles	172
	Reading the Oracle	181
16.	Dancing with the Ancestors: Cultivating Shamanic Experience	184
	Why Do We Say Shaman?	185
	Trance States for Extrasensory Perception	188
	Ask for Help from Your Spirit Guides	200

Conclusion: Re-Visioning the World One Dream at a Time	201
We Are the Storytellers	202
Changing Our Stories	203
Following Love – Re-Visioning Earth	208

List of Exercises	211
Reference Notes	213
Selected Reading	218
Acknowledgments	221
About the Author	223

Foreword

What joyful medicine this beautiful book by Liz Meacham is. If there is a more important undertaking at this point in history than reconnecting with the Earth, I don't know what it is. Were we to make a list of the most serious challenges confronting us today, most of them would trace back in one way or another to a deep cleavage between ourselves and nature, between our mind and the mind that gave birth to the universe. If there is a core deficit that threatens to engulf us, it is that we have lost contact with the life that lives in all things and so feel ourselves adrift in the infinite expanse of space and time.

In many ways our self-estrangement is no one's fault. Some would say it was even inevitable that in exercising our burgeoning capacities we would push ourselves away from that which holds us. We have dethroned so many gods, outgrown so many visions of what is true that our isolation feels like the inevitable cost of our self-advancement. Perhaps it is. And yet, as we rush headlong into the greatest extinction of life on this planet in 65 million years, as we deplete the oceans, drain our aquifers and destabilize our climate, we know that something is terribly wrong. Somewhere in our magnificent development we have lost something that we desperately need if we are to thrive here.

The many social, political and technological innovations we must enact in order to change the destructive course we are on will likely fail if they are not grounded in a deeper *experience* of our connection to the life that surrounds and sustains us. But how can we rekindle our sense of place and presence? How can we re-ground ourselves in the sacred spirituality of embodiment? This is where *Earth Spirit Dreaming* is so very helpful.

Liz Meacham is well versed in environmental philosophy and religious thought. She understands how we got here and has internalized the insights of the great eco-visionaries of our time. But it is in the practical exercises she offers in this remarkable book that we see her true genius. Here we see the light touch of a master of her form, sharing strategies of *embodied* awakening. She has refined and polished these practices through years of application and assessment, first in her university courses and then at the Lake Erie Institute in Cleveland, Ohio, which she founded and co-directs. These practices change lives.

I have always envied people who come into this world with a natural transparency to subtle dimensions. It's not been my gift, so I enjoy being around people like Liz who have this sensitivity wired in. What I especially love about Liz is how she translates her sensitivity into exercises that everyone can do. Through these simple practices we can begin to remember what we have forgotten, to recover what we have lost. There is nothing "paranormal" about them, she says. It is simply a matter of grounding ourselves more deeply in the touch and sound and pulse of nature. From here our boundaries slowly open, and we begin to engage with a larger life, an older life that is both us and more than us.

Earth Spirit Dreaming is deeply needed medicine for our times and a true gift to the world.

Christopher M. Bache, Ph.D.
Author of *Dark Night, Early Dawn* and
LSD and the Mind of the Universe

Part 1

Introduction

1

Introduction: Waking Up to Earth

Just before the fall equinox of 1995, I found Thomas Berry's book, *The Dream of the Earth*. His visionary environmental thinking ignited a profound longing to reconnect with life on Earth in ways that felt both new and remembered. In the first weeks of reading Berry's book, I found myself sitting in my yard, feeling every filament in my body with acute awareness. My entire nervous system seemed to connect through bands of light to the bands of energy emanating from the Earth. I felt acutely connected, as if I had finally come home. A line from a poem that I wrote that same week captures my experience:

> *I touch hand to dirt and grass, skin to skin our love replenishes me*
> *Our relationship I am lost in, identity fades and I am one*
> *Arches of light, arches of life, extension of your cosmic being*

Berry's book catalyzed a spiritual awakening in me. Many unexplainable experiences of awe in nature followed. I found that I could not categorize these experiences through the lens of traditional Western thinking. I began turning over many stones, literally and figuratively, to expand, and learn to share with others, these life-changing experiences. During the first decade of my eco-spiritual study and practice, I was working through childhood physical and emotional abuse by my mother. My nature based spiritual practices became an integral part of my healing. Lying on the Earth, immersing myself in rivers, meditating with rocks, I found safety and a sense of place within the web of the Earth community, though my human family remained painfully fractured. My yearning to contextualize these life-changing experiences took me to graduate school and the completion of my Ph.D, and then to work as a professor. I taught environmental studies through an experiential lens, often teaching in nature. I experienced shifts in myself and my students that went beyond what learning from books, and in classrooms, could offer. I discovered that teaching and learning through outdoor "spiritual" practices cultivated in my students a natural sensitivity to the Earth. More than just ideas, it was this inner shift that fostered an authentic environmental ethic of care. While much of environmental learning can be psychologically overwhelming, the Earth-connected spiritual experiences gave many of my students the hope and courage necessary to act for the Earth. Learning to feel their part in the web of life gave them sustenance to face the challenges of engaging in activism to heal the planet.

My work to foster Earth-care in others through experiential learning led to qualitative studies and careful experimentation. I wanted to find consistent teaching methods that could actualize profound moments of shift toward Earth-consciousness in my students. Through this research, I developed a combination of experiences that consistently encourages an opening to interrelationship with the Earth community. This method, entitled Earth Spirit Dreaming, is in three steps: Earth-connecting practices, Spirit-connection practices and Dream-connecting practices. Visionary environmental thinkers offer many ideas for restoring human connection with Earth systems. The Earth Spirit Dreaming method translates these transformative ideas into shamanic ecotherapy practices, making them accessible and applicable in everyday life. Further, the practices invite profound mindfulness, as we work to hold a vision of connection with the Earth and spirit realms, while choosing consciously to focus on joy, beauty, gratitude, love and healing.

From Earth-Connection to Earth-Care

The idea that we are interconnected with all life on Earth is becoming common knowledge. We understand that we are part of the larger ecological systems on the planet. We know that these systems must come into balance to remain viable for much of life on Earth. More and more people understand that we must respect and care for the "balance of nature."

However, after almost two centuries of increased industrialization, we are just beginning to realign our civilization with the Earth.

There are many books available today on why we need to restore our balance with nature, and many on how to "live green." These books include ideas such as using compact fluorescent light bulbs, shifting to a vegetarian diet, taking our own bags to the store and creating less trash. These kinds of actions are very important. They establish the moral commitment to living sustainably. Unfortunately, many of the "live green" books offer changes that are too small to get us where we need to be in terms of consumption to mitigate the global damage perpetrated by industrial civilization. Even if we do everything these books suggest, which leads to cutting our overall consumption almost in half, it is still not enough to keep our growing population within the limits of our Earth.[1] It is only through profound changes in our underlying meaning structures that we will muster the strength to make the necessary changes to maintain our home on Earth (note: Earth will go on with or without us).

Outside, "in the world" changes are an essential part of the puzzle of sustainability. Inside changes — the underlying beliefs and experiences of who we are in relation to each other and the Earth — are equally important, and too often overlooked. Western belief systems encourage a blind spot in our collective recognition of the depth of our interconnection with the Earth. We must shift our beliefs about what is meaningful and important to live sustainably. To become engaged citizens of a regenerative civilization, we need to align our psychological and spiritual selves with the rhythms of life: we must learn to live in ways that cultivate appreciation of our connection with Earth. Earth Spirit Dreaming offers one path to establish the awakened rootedness needed to become citizens of a whole planet. The step-by-step Earth Spirit Dreaming process guides the readers through a progressive actualization process toward integral connection with ourselves, each other and the planet.

Many environmental thinkers see reconnection with the Earth community as a path toward caring for the Earth community. Aldo Leopold, in his influential essay "The Land Ethic," argued that connecting with the land is essential to caring for the land.[2] Leopold took from Darwin the idea that human ethics evolved from the care inherent in human societies. According to Darwin, human survival depends on care relationships, such as those between mother and child. Darwin postulated that societies with better "rules" of care, or ethics of care, were stronger, thereby making ethics an essential element of furthering the species. Based on Darwin's view of ethics, Leopold reasoned that the development of an Earth ethic required fostering care for the Earth.

Deep ecologists Arne Naess and Joanna Macy, two influential environmental thinkers who came after Leopold, also value care for the Earth as the most important ingredient for an Earth ethic. Their notion of the ecological self, discussed in more detail in the next chapter, focuses on the need to identify the self with the Earth community as a form of self-actualization. The care developed through this connection with Earth, according to Naess, is the only means by which we will come back into balance with the Earth. Duty is not a strong enough impulse to make the necessary changes to live in balance with the Earth. Only seeing the Earth as an extension of ourselves will lead us back into balance with nature.

But how do we reconnect with Earth? Indigenous knowledges offer examples of social structures that foster ecological consciousness: Earth-consciousness. In Western culture, these forms of experience are often considered "extrasensory." What we think of as extrasensory experiences in Western culture, however, are considered a part of the normal sphere of reality in many indigenous cultures, and even in Western culture prior to the Enlightenment. To live in balance with the Earth, according to central environmental thinkers, we will need to realize these capacities once again to create a society that incorporates an Earth-honoring ethic.

Part of our task is to discover perceptual abilities that were written off as "primitive" by early ethnographers encountering indigenous cultures.[3] The increased interest in indigenous ways, and in "shamanism," represents an impulse to restore these lost modes of experience. *Earth Spirit Dreaming* offers practices to develop what we may think of in Western cultures as non-ordinary experiences that fit the common themes of shamanic cultures. We need to come back to our ancestral shamanic heritage: living lives deeply interwoven with the life-world, through "spiritual" modes, on a daily basis. In Berry's words from *The Dream of the Earth*:[4]

> *In moments of confusion such as the present, we are not left simply to our own rational contrivances. We are supported by the ultimate powers of the universe as they make themselves present to us through the spontaneities within our own being. We need only become sensitized to these spontaneities, not with a naïve simplicity, but with critical appreciation. This intimacy with our genetic endowment, and through this endowment with the larger cosmic process, is not primarily the role of the philosopher, priest, prophet, or professor. It is the role of the shamanic personality, a type that is emerging once again in our society.*
>
> *…Not only is the shamanic type emerging in our society, but also the shamanic dimensions of the psyche itself. In periods of significant cultural creativity, this aspect of the psyche takes on a pervasive role throughout the society and shows up in all the basic institutions and professions…*
>
> *This shamanic insight is especially important just now when history is being made not primarily within nations or between nations, but between humans and the Earth, with all its living creatures. In this context all our professions and institutions must be judged primarily by the extent to which they foster this mutually enhancing human—Earth relationship.*[5]

Slowing Down

An important first step to finding our way back to our Earth-connected, ecological selves is slowing down. We need to slow down. Do less. Be less. Make less. Produce less. Throw away less. Burn less. In the growth mindset of the industrial paradigm, more is believed to be better. The outcome of beliefs that press us to be and do more are that we are often sad and sick, disconnected from nature, our souls and each other. Many of us feel harried, trapped, lost and anxious on a daily basis.

Not only are we struggling to find health and balance in our overproducing world, we are also quickly eating up the resources of our finite planet. As Jennie Moore and William E. Rees put it in their article "Getting to One-Planet Living," we are in "ecological overshoot — requiring the equivalent of 1.5 planets to provide the renewable resources we use and to absorb our carbon waste."[6] These authors ask, how do we get to one-planet living? They offer a variety of "in the world" solutions. The question often arises among environmental thinkers: why is it so hard to make these kinds of changes? Is it the force of habit, culture, overwhelm, the media, the human tendency toward laziness? We know what we need to do, yet we don't seem to be able to do it. We need to shift our underlying meaning systems to revolutionize our habits.

Attempting to slow down can bring up many profound fears as we break away from values and belief systems that have guided our nations, communities and even families for decades or, in some cases, centuries. One current and powerful underlying motivation is to organize our lives to make money. We could change this to growing food, to healing, to being together. Often, many of these other things are made to fit around our need to make money: the primary medium of exchange in our culture. While it is difficult to imagine, there are alternatives to living within a linear economic mindset.

What we need are methods to retrain our ways of being in the world; but the level of change required can only occur with an accompanying spirituality. All civilizations have had systems of ritual that support and perpetuate beliefs, and underpin the courage needed to act for these beliefs under duress.

A regenerative civilization requires a system of ritual, a spirituality, as well. As a global movement, this spirituality must be applicable across diverse cultural and religious beliefs. Dolores LaChapelle, in her now-famous article "Ritual is Essential,"[7] points out the following regarding Earth-centered cultures:

> *Most native societies around the world had three common characteristics: they had an intimate, conscious relationship with their place; they were stable "sustainable" cultures, often lasting for thousands of years; and they had a rich ceremonial and ritual life. They saw these three as intimately connected.* [8]

This book focuses on methods to achieve the first and third elements that LaChapelle suggests are required to live in balance with the Earth: a conscious relationship with our place and a rich ceremonial and ritual life. *Earth Spirit Dreaming* is a manual that offers methods for reanimating our intimacy with the Earth by filling our personal lives and communities with nature-focused ceremony and ritual.

Earth Spirit Dreaming: Three Steps for Re-Visioning Our Planetary Stories

In my teaching, I develop and work with a variety of Earth-connected spiritual practices. Evaluating these practices through qualitative studies, I have developed three progressive phases of practices that effectively grow Earth-connected sensitivities. While there are many different practices available to complete each step, the combination of the steps consistently creates a shift in perspective, which produces experiences of healing and rebalancing within the web of life. Even after short rituals, students and workshops attendees consistently express surprise at their very new kinds of perceptions. In my longer workshops and trainings, people marvel at the expansion of their non-cognitive and intuitive intelligence. They discover magic and wonder in interwoven waves of what I think of as meta-synchronicities; flashes of the underlying non-linear, non-local vibrational fabric of the universe. Things begin to happen that cross the boundaries of time and space. Recently, a student said, "You did something to me. My dreams are so wild now." I didn't do anything. It's waking up to our genetic sensitivities to the Earth and spirit realms — waking up from separation — that changes lives. And Earth Spirit Dreaming is only one way to make these kinds of shifts.

It is the story of the way that came forth in my own internally guided search for an indigenous experience in connection with the Earth that I know: where I live and eat and grow. There are many other paths and resources for waking up to an Earth-honoring way of life, some of which I will refer to throughout this book.

I call the three steps of Earth Spirit Dreaming Earth-connecting, Spirit-connecting and Dream-connecting. In the first step, Earth-connecting practices help readers develop an awareness of embodied connection with the Earth community through mindfulness of our source. Consistent practice of Earth-connecting rituals opens doorways to what we think of in Western culture as "altered" states of consciousness, or extrasensory perception. These states of consciousness lead to the next step in the process, which is spirit-connecting. In this book, spiritual connection means experiences of being part of something larger than ourselves that take us to the level of awe. From this numinous orientation, the practices in this book encourage the reader to develop a sensitivity to webs of connection perceived through Western language and concepts as the subtle energies, or vibrations, underlying all of life. These webs are overlapping, co-creative dreams stemming from the stories of all expressions of consciousness in the universe.

It's important to note that what we define in our culture as energy, or vibrational reality — this numinous reality that we often feel in flashes of wonder that feel magical and somehow beyond us — has never been an abnormal perception. It was present in early humans and is still present in many modern indigenous societies.[9] In indigenous cultures, perception of "spirits" often means something different than it does in Western cultures. Spirit can be a way of explaining a normal part of life, rather than a different form of reality. This "spirit" realm is, in part, an expression of aliveness: a sensitivity to the energetic imprint of other beings.

In the third step, the dream-connecting practices guide readers through practices that awaken the symbolic realms of experience. Dreaming, in the lexicon of this book, can be understood as a form of visioning. Some indigenous cultures refer to visioning, or creating reality through focusing on certain things and living into the realm of stories, as dreaming. Through the dream-connecting practices, readers are invited to relate to the imaginal realms in ways that are often limited by a focus on rational thinking. The dreaming, or visioning, exercises in this book support understanding of the role of focus and creative visualization in shifting our lives and the world. Dreaming in this method also asks of us a new level of commitment to living mindfully with our own stories, which inform all of our beliefs and actions whether we are conscious of them or not. Dreaming for the healing of the Earth requires unprecedented, moment-by-moment attention to what we think and feel as a result of our stories — personal, familial, cultural, global — and how these stories inform our creation of reality as we know it. Awake dreaming is not for the faint of heart; it can be rigorous, wild, surprising, painful, exhilarating beyond imagining. And, it often takes us beyond boundaries that we previously did not know existed. Becoming conscious dreamers is an initiation, and a way to become fully human; it is a path to engaging with the world as harbingers of a healing planetary consciousness.

Earth-Connecting Practices

The Earth-connecting practices offered in this book reconnect us with our bodies and the Earth. Our bodies hold sensitivities that allow us to consciously engage with the Earth community. Reconnecting with nature, and with our bodies, enlivens dormant, often atrophied, senses. Rediscovering what ecopsychologist Michael J. Cohen calls "natural senses"[10] helps us to become mindful of the web of relationships that surrounds us in every moment of our lives. These practices focus particularly on the ecological web of relationships that we rely on for life on Earth.

Understanding insights from ecology can transform our individual lives. The single most important idea from ecological thought is that everything is connected. While this idea can be expanded upon with great detail, the central seed of the idea is that everything can best be known and understood in relationship. Ecology deals with the study of organisms in relation to one another, and to their environment. Translated to a personal level, ecology tells us that, as it is in nature, so it is in our own lives; in an ecological framework, we can understand *ourselves* best in the composition of our own environment. The social sciences, and psychology, contextualize human life within our human environments. Visionary ecological thought tells us that to be in balance with the Earth, we must understand and develop healthy relationships within our more-than-human environment as well. Humans are part of nature, but we are only one part. Cutting ourselves off from the whole of life on Earth, and only focusing on a small part, the human world, has created profound imbalances for our species and the planet.

Combining ecological thought with mindfulness, we can learn to focus on and become present to our ecological reality. Deep ecologists call this capacity the ecological self. I consider this a form of spiritual development, as the experience of the ecological self creates consciousness of our part in something larger than ourselves. For framing of the practices in this book, we can think of this larger "self" on Earth as Gaia. People refer to Earth as Gaia for a variety of reasons, including spiritual, archetypal and scientific to name a few. In Greek mythology, Gaia is Earth personified in the form of a goddess, the ancestral mother of all life on the planet. Scientist James Lovelock, in his now famous Gaia Hypothesis, argues that the biosphere is a self-regulating organism that organizes and perpetuates all planetary systems.[11] Lovelock's Gaia Hypothesis helped transform the destructive, industrial model of the Earth, which conceives of nature existing primarily for our use. His thinking supports an ecological model of nature by showing that the Earth has her own ends and intrinsic value, which require our honor and respect.

I incorporate mindfulness techniques in many of the practices that develop ecological consciousness because they offer simple and proven ways to slow down the mind and awaken the senses. Mindfulness, like fields in philosophy such as phenomenology, invites us to live deeply into the present moment. What I call "ecomindfulness" employs mindfulness techniques to help us live deeply into our ecology. Because we are part of nature, we do not need to be in natural settings as they are commonly understood to become more present to the role of nature in our lives.

Nature is our lives. We are nature. Nature is with us every moment: in our breath, our blood, our cells, the water we partake of and are made up of, our use of stored sun as energy and all of our life processes, inside and out. We are life and cannot exist without the complex matrices of life. Becoming mindful of this and learning to hold the reality of embeddedness in nature is undoubtedly easier if, at first, we take ourselves to a beautiful place "out in nature," in the sense of unspoiledness that we tend to associate with "natural" places. As we grow in this ability, we find that we are in fact "in nature" at all times and in all places; but some places are more degraded by human insensitivity and overuse than others. As we wake up our mindfulness and aesthetic connection to the patterns and design of "nature," places that have been overtaken by the human mind and that have no proper balance with nature can start to feel very dead and can elicit strong feelings of sadness and grief. These feelings of grief are, though, part of ecomindfulness and are an essential element of the process of reclaiming our birthright as humans: understanding and *sensing on all levels of our being* our place in the web of life. Joanna Macy's work, discussed more in the next chapter, addresses the importance of this process of grief in our waking up to the world.

Spirit-Connecting Practices

The second step of Earth Spirit Dreaming requires practices that deepen our spiritual perceptivity. Many of the practices in the Earth- and body-connecting work above can also be defined as spiritual. They include creating a sense of the sacred in our lives, learning to foster awe and reconnecting with the Earth community. The Earth Spirit Dreaming practices use the reawakened sensitivities to the natural world that are developed in the first step to support working with energetic and vibrational reality. In order to "dream," or to vision, from a frame of mind that is conducive to connection and healing, we must first learn to clear ourselves of destructive "vibrational" entanglements. There are many ways to understand unhealthy entanglements that do not require thinking in terms of energetic, or vibrational, reality. For the goals of this book, it is important to learn to understand and work with these kinds of experiences, even if they seem "not real." In fact, it's equally useful to only "imagine" that we are working with energy and vibrations. Imagination is an essential tool for reconnecting with and re-dreaming our world. Through visualization and imagination, we can open to life-changing experiences of oneness. Often, our minds cannot follow where our bodies and hearts lead. Our minds are ill-equipped to act as containers of relational consciousness. Yet, "the watcher," the fully integrated, multidimensional consciousness that each of us has, can support the profundities of relational reality. It is through re-threading ourselves within the weave of the matrix of life that we move into our full capacities as humans. The spirit-connecting rituals of Earth Spirit Dreaming are one of many ways to reseat our consciousness into our fully sensing and energetic bodies to consciously affect change in vibrational reality.

As we slow down and connect with nature, our nature and the nature all around us, even in the city, we can find our way to an innate knowledge of subtle realms that many people in Western culture have forgotten. As we tune in to these realms of vibration, we can learn to clear vibrations that hold us in thrall to ways of living, creating and dreaming that are out of balance with our own well-being and the Earth. Our soul self, the self that exists as part of something larger than our ego, wants to live in balance, peace and harmony with all of life on Earth and in the cosmos. Coming into alignment with the Earth helps to bring us into alignment with this soul self, where we find a sense of balance, fulfillment, peace and purpose previously unknown to us. While we can still acknowledge great sadness for the pain of the world, we can find a way to create harmony through visioning health and life-giving energy for all beings and for the planet. We learn to become conduits of healing for life, rather than pulling energy from life and continuing to drain the resources of the spirit of Earth.

Typically, without knowing it, many of us are pulling energy into ourselves with unconscious wanting, needing and taking. Even if we have done a lot of work on ourselves, and are relatively psychologically healthy, the habit of mind, body and heart that comes from the dominant global culture encourages us to fear, to strive, to worry and to plan for our survival — to pull energy into ourselves. This habit is often so ingrained that it requires daily practice and continual vigilance, as well as a lot of soul searching, to learn another way: to be in a position of energy-giver rather than taker. As we work on this, though, we can begin to stay in a place that allows us to live and to dream our reality from a place of trust, joy and gratitude.

Dream-Connecting Practices

As mentioned above, what we most often think of as "visualization" in Western culture is thought of as "dreaming" in some indigenous cultures. In this context "dreaming" is a form of co-creation in our daily lives (a related concept in Buddhism is the idea of dependent co-arising). Groups such as the Pachamama Alliance see changing our collective dream in Western culture as essential to healing our world. According to the indigenous elders who inspire the work of the Pachamama Alliance, what we see and envision, we create. In keeping with this indigenous perspective, I'm referring to visioning as dreaming, since I too believe that our lives on Earth are in some sense a dream, or a collection of stories, that we can heal and change.

What does it mean to heal the dream of the Earth? First, to own our power for creating life as it is. We have tremendous power, through every thought and action, to create the dream that we live in. This idea can seem beyond irrational, and even crazy, to the Western-trained mind. We are taught to believe that reality is objective, something that exists "out there" and on its own. The ecological paradigm teaches us that, since everything is connected, reality is essentially relational and thus malleable along the porous borders and criss-crossed patterns that exist between forms of life. We know from Heisenberg's uncertainty principle, from the field of quantum physics, that we are always partaking in how reality appears to us. The dense, physical reality all around us is made up of the collective dream of many people, and the planet, over long periods of time. To dream a new way of life into being, we must collectively wake up and "come to our senses."

Those of us who consciously work for the healing of the world encounter seemingly endless people pouring their care and creativity into healing the world in remarkable ways. There are millions of organizations all over the world, each, in their own diverse ways, connecting with their own land and people, cultivating local economies, growing their own food and working for social justice. Paul Hawken, in his book *Blessed Unrest: How the Largest Social Movement in History Is Restoring Grace, Justice, and Beauty to the World*,[12] chronicles this rapidly growing movement. Hawken identifies the power of small, individual changes when seen as a web of change encompassing the planet:

> *How do we sow our seeds when large, well-intentioned institutions and intolerant ideologies that purport to be our salvation cause so much damage? One sure way is through smallness, grace, and locality. Individuals start where they stand and, in Antonio Machado's poetic dictum, make the road by walking.*[13]

Rather than ceding the power to create the vision of the world to those who we think of as "in power," the Earth Spirit Dreaming practices encourage us to become lucid dreamers creating a new story of justice, peace, harmony, creativity, beauty and love. We can create a new dream that honors all of life at every level. Sound like a "pipe dream?" Yes, maybe sacred pipes, and indigenous ways, can help us get there. In every pocket of pain and darkness on the planet, there are blooming lights of dreamers building a web of transformation. We are a web of light, working for life; we are creating a healing dream for the Earth.

2

How to Use This Book: Growing the Gifts of Ecological Consciousness

Earth Spirit Dreaming is both a manual and a memoir; it is a guide through the many practices that opened me to ecological consciousness and a personal story of discovering pathways to re-indigenizing my own mind. The journey for Western people to find our way back to the Earth is not done once, but over and over again, beginning fresh each day. As we grow communities and cultural rituals that support ecological consciousness, and as I live into these practices and groups of people for longer periods of time, maintaining an ecologically embedded experience of life gets easier and lasts longer. As it is, daily commitment and practice is required to foster the emergence of Earth sensitivities and consciousness.

My hope for anyone reading this book is that you will find steps to re-indigenize your own mind, and to cultivate community with others to do the same. Because feeling separate, when we really are not, is a central fallacy of Western ideology, coming back to the Earth is always more easily and powerfully done together. Whatever inner calling led you to this book — personal growth, a longing for Earth-based spiritual practice alone or with others, developing shamanic sensitivities, teaching, facilitating, leadership and/or just wanting ways to love Earth more intimately — my intention is that, through the variety of exercises and diversity of combinations, most people who discover this book will find some way to integrate Earth Spirit Dreaming into their life and work.

There are many practices in the book for each step of the Earth Spirit Dreaming method. The goal of the book is to guide readers to piece the practices together to reach states that support communion with nature, immersions with vibrational reality and direct contact with helping spirits and the planetary light guides. The practices in this book can be utilized by anyone interested in developing an experiential, spiritual approach to an Earth-connected life. The book is designed to be accessible and relevant for individuals developing or enhancing a personal spiritual practice, as well as for groups, facilitators, clergy, religious educators, healing practitioners, teachers and professors. The practices and method are adaptable to a variety of settings, and can be used in many different situations, modes and locations. The book can also be used as a manual to lead practitioners and facilitated groups, chapter by chapter, through progressive learning experiences and spiritual growth.

The book is set up to offer a dynamic course of study that moves through the development of increased ecological consciousness from chapter to chapter. The exercises in the book can be used intermittently, integrated into already established spiritual praxis, or be used in order as a stand-alone path for integrated spiritual development. While the practices can be enjoyed separately, eventually, to reach Earth Spirit Dreaming states, they need to be done regularly and consistently, and in a particular order. For example, consistent spiritual experience requires consistent and increasing commitment to contemplative practices over time. Also, while we choose the next step, we are always evolving in relation to the world and the cosmos, so we must make our commitment to practicing with care and commitment while releasing the results to the Divine. We can bring ourselves to the doorway of experience, but it is through shared agreement and relationship that the doorways open for us to pass through to new levels of experience.

Working with This book

There are many ways to experience and move through this book, and they are not mutually exclusive. The first three chapters introduce readers to the Earth Spirit Dreaming method and the format of the book. Chapter Three offers a brief introduction to the visionary environmental thought that inspired and supports my own work. Reading that is optional, but probably useful for anyone who is new to these ideas or wants to teach or facilitate the work with others. The following sections of the book provide a context and practice for each step in the method: earth-connecting, spirit-connecting and dream-connecting.

It is up to you to decide how much time to spend with *Earth Spirit Dreaming*; there is value in any amount of time that we spend reconnecting with our Earth and Spirit sensitivities. As I've been practicing and teaching these methods for decades, I've come to see the value in years, months, days, hours, or even minutes of exploration with various combinations of these practices. You can jump right in, pick one or a few practices from each section and put them together in order to create a ceremony for yourself or for or with a group. When creating experiences for others, I highly recommend that you spend time with the practices to help you understand the sometimes surprising shifts and feelings that can arise as we wake up to life in new ways. Expect occasional sudden floods of feelings and flashes of unusual perceptions, and learn how to "come back" from these moments to re-enter the "normal" world. When facilitating, you will need to support others through these kinds of experiences, so it's important to find your own ways of managing these moments and transitions. When in doubt, know that the Earth and the helping spirits are always there to guide us. Whether or not you feel the presence of any spirits or ancestors, or even if you do not believe in anything, you can always pray and ask for help from the Divine Spirit of the Universe, and ask for guidance from the helping spirits. Even when our minds and hearts feel very blocked, or we feel lost and alone, we can always speak to the Earth and ask for help. I always ask the Earth and Divine Spirit to guide me in my practice and teaching. We are part of concentric circles of collective wisdom and never have to move through rituals, or teaching and facilitating, on our own. One important thing to do is to find others to talk to about Earth- and Spirit-connected awareness as they grow in your life. We need to reclaim and rebuild a nomenclature for eco-shamanic experience that captures and helps us express the wonders and mystery that surface. When I lead groups, I find that most people have experiences of contact with nature, spirit, guides and ancestors. Building language around them in community brings them more and more to the "front" of our psyche.

As you approach this book, begin as you feel most inspired. It is a book that can be read in many different ways and is not meant to be a "front to back" read. Turn the pages until something speaks in your heart and start there, no matter what section you are in. Then, build a ritual around it using at least one practice from each section. Doing any Earth Spirit Dreaming ritual that you create, for just 15 minutes a day, will transform your life. An hour a day, or over many days, with these practices may shift the course of your life, as it has mine. We hear the guides more clearly with every moment that we practice with commitment, and more practice eventually brings us into community. Eventually, through mindfulness of our connection with life, we will well and truly do our part to shift the consciousness of our global culture toward regenerative, life-supporting, Earth-honoring ways.

Daily Practice of Rituals

Shifting consciousness requires daily practice. *Earth Spirit Dreaming* suggests many exercises, from the very small to the long and large, that can fit into our lives whenever and wherever possible. The most important thing is commitment to doing something to connect with the Earth every day. Some days we have a moment, some days we can take the entire day or more. If we find rituals that fit our lives, our schedules and our own intentions, we will be able to find time for these rituals even in very busy and sometimes difficult times. These small moments add up over time and open our minds to more connection and the ability to slow down and shift more often and more quickly into the emerging indigenization that grows over time from small steps. For any of us, larger shifts eventually come from the small; and for me, I often begin from a sense of estrangement and separation, and I start again and again, because this is the challenge of our era: to claw our way out of the myth of separation. It is work that is done, not one time, but over and over again. Even for those of us who make this the work of our lifetime it is still a constant challenge to maintain our ecological consciousness and come back again and again to Earth.

For everyone, no matter what your calling or vocation, there is room in your life to become part of creating an Earth-honoring civilization. This book offers a wide variety of practices that can fit many lifestyles and intentions, and many kinds of work. Small practices once a day lead to big changes, and all of our work matters and grows as we do it together, whether we know of the many, many others who are doing similar work or not. As you engage the Earth Spirit Dreaming method, allow your heart to guide you to the places in this book that fit your life. Discover and create rituals that are meaningful and supportive within the framework of your own days. How much time, how many rituals and how quickly we feel shifts is not important with Earth Spirit Dreaming. These are messages of achievement and linear progress that are pressures from the culture that we wish to grow out of. Eventually, Earth Spirit Dreaming takes us out of linear notions of progress and achievement. We realize that we are all together across space, non-linear and non-local, *becoming*: together in labyrinthine complexity, so that my hand touching this tree for one moment is equal to the birth of a star on the other side of the galaxy. With this trust in the miracle of life, we can be soft and kind with ourselves, beginning when, how and where we feel safety and support.

A Method for Discovering Magic

I developed Earth Spirit Dreaming as a method because I found through my own long-time spiritual practice, and work with others, that using the steps in order consistently creates shifts toward experiential integration with all of life. To create an Earth Spirit Dreaming ritual for yourself, first familiarize yourself with the exercises in each chapter; this can be a quick flip through looking for words, phrases or ideas that catch your eye. Certain exercises will feel like a better fit for you than others. You can also modify the exercises to fit within your own spiritual, religious or other regular practices. Because we are essentially creative beings at our core, each person's path to connect with Earth and spirit realms will be different. That said, there are steps, or protocols, that support moving into these levels of experience that maintain similarities over millennia.

So, while we may "write our own book," we use a common language and an alphabet of Earth-connected "shamanic" experience.

Over time, and with consistent practice, the Earth Spirit Dreaming method opens us to a journey of spirals deepening into Mystery. More and more, we let go of rational understanding and enter into a new world of sensations. Though our minds cannot conceive of the non-linear reality of "magical" experience, we continue to develop our means of relating with this holonic consciousness.[14] Daily practice turns into weeks, months, years — and suddenly, at first in glimpses, and then sometimes in long and winding waves, we find that we are experiencing the magical, non-linear, out-of-time, emergent creative miracle of the life-world. "Ah," some part of us long forgotten says, "this is magic!"

You may — and this is my hope and intention — feel and discover strange and exciting new parts of yourself and our world. Through regular practice, I've discovered "portals" to ancient Earth memories, ancestors, wild energies of the plants and animals around me, shimmering with shift and light that I've never known or seen before. I sometimes run away in fear, and often remember that these miracles are best experienced with friends. Together, in wisdom, we weave our stories and trust the spirit helpers and ancestors to be our guides. I now know that I have a "portal" in my heart. Sometimes, with help from great light guides, my heart opens and I fall through myself and into the cosmos. Sometimes, it feels like too much in a given moment and I'm not ready. I gently say "no." We have agency to manage these relationships and to set the boundaries and pace that feel comfortable for us. However you choose to follow this path, know that I share my story, as it is expressed through this method, with the deepest hope and longing for everyone to feel the beauty and connection, the constant miracles, that Earth and Spirit have shared with me.

Because I want so deeply to share these states of wonder, and because the method captures how my own unfolding into expanded consciousness occurs, I've planned the stages of this book to progressively amplify awareness through what are often considered "altered states" of consciousness.

Really, these are re-indigenized states that occur as we revive our Earth and Spirit sensitivities. Reconnecting with our evolutionary capacity to work with elemental nature energies and vibrational reality, we set the stage to contact and communicate with spirit helpers and ancestors that exist around the Earth interwoven and overlapping with reality as we know it. Though we tend to think of "angels" or helping spirits as being "out there" and distant from us, really they are just a thin veil away in each moment. The challenge is to shift the orientation of consciousness to connect with them and receive the help that we need to heal and transform our lives and our world.

Prepare, Prepare, Prepare

In our culture slowing down enough to prepare our mental, physical and emotional containers for spiritual development is particularly challenging and, for this reason, all the more essential. The Earth Spirit Dreaming method prepares us to enter sometimes intense realms of experience with care and conscious awareness, and most importantly with helping spirits to guide us. Great care is required to not re-create from the consciousness that got us into this mess, but to forge a new path of visioning. In this way, Earth Spirit Dreaming acts as one protocol of clarity, protection and navigation as we become fully engaged participants in ushering forth a new dream for the Earth.

I cannot emphasize enough that to create real change in the world through spiritual work we must prepare, prepare, prepare. If you undertake, for example, a shamanic journey, careful preparation in the time that you have is more important than the time spent on the visioning process. As your practice grows, you will develop methods, locations and practices that can more quickly get you to the correct orientation for healing work. At the beginning, preparation is most important. The helping spirits can communicate outside of time and space, and can download information very quickly. However, it may take days, months and years to create the circumstances to allow this communication to come through, and to unpack it, as has been the case for me.

Coming Home

The Earth Spirit Dreaming practices are a map of my own story of healing and transformation. I dedicate my story, and all that I share in this book, to the healing of all of our lives and the world. Together, we can find our way back to our heritage of Earth and Spirit connectedness. As I tell my story, I know that it goes against many of the things we value in our culture. Much of it may seem irrational or even crazy, and much of it is based on ways of knowing that are not situated in fact but derive from subjective experience. Mine is a story of unfolding soul and spirit in a culture that struggles to find its way back to these modes of experience. I did not go to others to learn this way of being but found my way on the soil beneath my feet in the United States of America, living a Western life and reading books written largely by Western, and often white male, thinkers. But my experience is one that is happening throughout Western culture: a breaking through of our cellular memory of ways of living and knowing that we need now to effectively resolve the challenges that we face as a planetary community.

Everything that I share in this book is a gift from the Earth, from the helping spirits, from the Divine Creator of the Universe. My wish for myself, and for all of us, is to be an emissary of life power to wake up the people to reclaim our birthright of creative connection and to walk in beauty on the planet. I came to this knowledge and intention by sitting with Earth, speaking directly with Gaia, asking for direction and learning to read the mysterious and, many times, magical feeling of the messages as they come in imaginal and symbolic ways. My guides and I have developed methods for communication over many years.

In every day that passes, I am surprised by life. There is always another circle of discovery and magic to stretch and grow into. As I continue my journey, which is often a struggle, to maintain awareness of my ecology, I continue to face the challenges of sitting with this knowing alongside techno-industrial consciousness. I find recently that there is a new feeling-quality to this experience of walking between worlds. That as I move every day closer to the Earth, I begin to feel the vibrational matrix of life more often and in more and different places: not just in the woods or meditating with my rocks, but at the coffee shop, in my kitchen, while driving; or in the city, in the grocery store, late at night in my bed. I want to describe this feeling, but words elude me. It is a world, a consciousness, a feeling experience that is not slower, but slower is the only word that is close. It's like a broad long, constant, slow wave amidst short colliding waves.

The feeling of the web of life is usually soft. While sometimes these experiences of oneness can be large, jolting, mind-splitting, I find that the everyday feeling of connecting with the web of life is quiet. It is like a very soft whisper in a room of people talking loudly. If I'm not paying attention I won't hear it; if I don't consciously wake up the parts of me that can feel it, it can easily slip under the brighter, noisier, busier perceptions of the dream of techno-industrial human culture. In my life and work, I increasingly try to hold both at once. This is challenging, as the attractions and pressures of the human culture world are very engaging and often hold my attention rapt. It's almost like listening to two kinds of music at once. While these songs can go together, they can also clash and hurt.

In these moments, I focus on connection with the Earth, and on love. Love can shift thousands of moments of weighted fear and other negative emotions. We are not left to flail in a think-soup of loneliness and longing. Now more than ever the great light guides of the planet, and the depths of our own humanity, are calling us back to ourselves, to reclaim our home of beauty and love on Earth. We can close the gap of separation with ourselves and others as we share our joys, our grief, our fears, our dreams in circles of care. We learn to give our feelings to the Earth, all of them. To be reconstituted into the consciousness of the planet. We compost these feelings through contact with the Earth, always with requests for permission and profound gratitude.

To change the world, most, if not all, of us will need to commit to an Earth-connecting practice of some sort, because while culture is expressed outside of us, it originates within and among us in the embodied psycho-spiritual fabric of community. We can only grow an

Earth-honoring culture by learning to honor the Earth again. In my personal experience, reaping the unexpected and life-changing gifts of Earth-connected consciousness began by feeling my way along, literally, amidst rocks and trees. Touching the Earth regularly, I had what I thought was a peak awakening, until I started to speak to the Earth and all of the community of life and engage through creative, intuitive ritual practice. This brought me to new peak awakenings, which, when I did these things first with just a couple of people, and eventually more and more, opened onto completely new horizons. Eventually, my goal, my hope, became to be a part of the shift on Earth that is healing through re-indigenizing Western minds. At some point it dawned on me: this isn't just something that might happen far off in the distance; it is happening now, in these circles, speaking with nature, touching the Earth in ceremony, sharing stories around fires, allowing our experience to move beyond our individual minds into collective awareness of the energetic fabric that holds us all in the matrix of life.

3

Everything Is Connected: A Brief Introduction to Visionary Environmental Thought

My personal mindfulness experiences in nature — watching myself and the nature of my mind while I watch, say, a river — allow me to see myself much more clearly. Like the river, my mind is a flow that moves uniquely, yet consistently, over the same bumps and crevices. Like the river, the movements of my mind become well-known to me. When we watch water, we don't know exactly how the water will look. Water is endlessly creative and always moves uniquely, but we know that unless it is stopped, we can count on it flowing over the same rocks. Watching ourselves amidst the ambiance of nature rituals, seeing ourselves reflected in the river, the tree, the bug, the wind, the sun, helps us reconnect with the natural rhythms that are the basic structure of our being and experience. On a psychological and cultural level, the core truth of ecology, that an organism can only be understood in the context of our natural environment, is equally true of the human person. On a spiritual level, understanding our primary connection and responsibility to our natural environment is essential to understanding our ethical tasks as individuals and communities.

My experience with rivers is beautifully reflected in the currents of awe that mingle with theory in Western visionary environmental thought. The single most important, and awe-inspiring, idea from the past century of environmental thought can be expressed in one deceptively simple maxim: everything is connected. This is both a philosophical idea and an opportunity for experiencing ourselves in new ways that shift our underlying beliefs, thereby transforming our actions. By fostering the relational senses that flow from the realization that everything is connected, we move toward re-indigenized ways of knowing. By following the trail of our own intellectual evolution, we resume our ancestral sense of belonging and place on a local, planetary and cosmic scale. As we live into the truth that everything is connected, the locus of personal and communal meaning begins to shift.

As a thinker and teacher, I am most influenced by these streams in environmental thought: participatory thinking, deep ecology, spiritual ecology and ecopsychology. While my work derives from Western thought, it is important to acknowledge that Anglo-environmental thought is deeply influenced by Eastern spiritual perspectives and indigenous ways of knowing. While I call the thinkers discussed in this chapter the *theoretical* basis of my work, and they certainly are, they are also poets singing the glory of the natural world and the cosmos. Scholarly writing often transitions to sacred reverence for the Earth in the pages of the books I will mention, capturing the reawakening of the Western mind to the enchantment of the world.

A Shifting Sense of Self: From Separation to Care and Connection

Our actions emanate from who we think we are. Our sense of ourselves, our beliefs about our SELF, are so ingrained that we rarely stop to examine them. Even if we do take the time to explore our beliefs about ourselves, many of the most basic assumptions and values that underlie our experience are not visible to us; they are deeply embedded in the historical and cultural belief systems of our families, communities and nations. These matrices of beliefs intersect with, and offer avenues to express, instinctual needs, longings and desires. These belief systems change over time, albeit usually quite slowly.

It is argued by many Western environmental thinkers that our current psychological and ethical stance toward the biosphere and other species is evolving, shifting the ingrained Western sense of a separate, delineated self. Specifically, the idea that human needs should come before the needs of the natural world and other species is no longer assumed. The idea that Western people are superior to the Earth, human "others," other creatures and natural cycles is changing. Increasingly, in public discourse, it is no longer presumed that the natural world is something to be used primarily to human advantage. The ethics of human rights are an important legacy of the 20th century. Environmental thinkers broaden this concern to consider the possibility of "rights" for natural beings, species, ecosystems and the planet.

Ecotheologian and historian Thomas Berry is a fulcrum point of the environmental ideas that I discuss in this chapter. He offered a now famous readjustment of Western thinking that captures the evolution of the idea of the Western "self," as well as the dominant ethical stance toward nature. One of his most famous ideas, repeated throughout his work, captures with profound wisdom and simplicity the shift that is required to heal our relationship with the Earth community; he suggests that to transform into an ecological age, we must begin to see the world as a communion of subjects, rather than a collection of objects.

Here is an example of Berry's use of this phrase from his book, *The Great Work*: "These spontaneities express the inner value of each being in such a manner that we must say of the universe that it is a communion of subjects, not a collection of objects."[15] Berry's work quickens the heart and stirs the soul to rediscover the beauty of the Earth. Like Emerson and the American transcendentalists, Berry is committed to translating an Earth ethic through the sublime. Though Berry's work isn't the beginning or the end of visionary environmental thought, his work moves the field toward an ethic of care for the Earth by acknowledging the sacred awe required to care for all of life.[16]

In Western culture, we begin learning that the world is a "collection of objects"[17] from a very young age. This is a result of the defining Cartesian/Newtonian mechanistic worldview that has dominated Western consciousness for more than 400 years. The Western SELF, in this framework, is a separate entity existing in a world of separate entities. I am reminded of an example from my son's early years that illustrates the mechanistic worldview quite well. At the age of three, my son said to my husband, "What is the universe made of?" My husband answered, "Atoms, molecules, electrons, tiny units of energy." I said, "That is what we learned in school, but is it really true?" Though it was likely annoying for my husband, I suggested that we could view the world instead as made up of interacting relationships of energy, another idea we learn in school. Why do we tend to focus on the separate entities that we believe to be the "building blocks" of the universe rather than the energetic relationships between them?

Another way to answer this kind of question is to focus on a relational model of reality: not to describe the individual parts, but to focus on the relationships and interactions that make up our world and the universe. What this story illustrates is our ingrained tendency, in Western cultures, to experience ourselves and understand reality as a "collection of objects," or in other words, from an atomistic perspective. The reason we do this is a long and complex story that requires grappling with the history of Western thought (which is beyond the scope of this book). Suffice to say, for the moment, that our Western belief structures give us the impression that we are separate individual "selves" moving around and among separate individual "selves." It comes as a surprise to many people indoctrinated into Western thinking that not all people on the Earth experience their "selves" this way. In fact, the notion of a separate self is only one way of experiencing life, which has pluses, and many minuses.

Delving into environmental thought and spirituality provides alternative perspectives for understanding our "selves" in relationship with others, the world and the cosmos. To face the challenges of our age, we need methods for developing new beliefs and patterns of living through the wisdom that is available by reconnecting with the Earth community. Environmental thinkers provide one path to these new ways of thinking and being by helping us understand our connections with all of life. As one of the early thinkers in Western environmental thought, Ralph Waldo Emerson championed the essential spiritual experience of nature as the core of an ethical relationship to the land. These famous words from his essay, "Nature," capture this well:

Standing on the bare ground, my head bathed by the blithe air, and uplifted into infinite space, all mean egotism vanishes.

I become a transparent eyeball; I am nothing; I see all; the currents of the Universal Being circulate through me; I am part or particle of God...

I am the lover of uncontained and immortal beauty. In the wilderness, I find something more dear and connate than in streets or villages. In the tranquil landscape, and especially in the distant line of the horizon, man beholds somewhat as beautiful as his own nature. (Nature, 1836, 10)[18]

The Participatory Worldview

We begin to assimilate the worldview of objects very young. We get the idea from what we are taught about ourselves: that we are separate entities existing in a world of separate entities. Reductionism, or the idea that things can best be understood by breaking them into their individual parts, is being replaced within certain strata of environmental thought. The scientific and philosophical field of ecology presents a worldview in which experience and the world can best be understood through complex webs of relationship. Participatory thought, an important offshoot of environmental thought from the last century, supports the idea that the world is relational, rather than atomistic and mechanistic.

The aspects of ourselves that develop in an atomistic worldview are very different from those that develop in a relational worldview. In the context of our evolution, we have existed as a species within a relational world view much longer than we have in an atomistic one. The ideas that support the experience of a separate self can be traced back to many thinkers in Western history, including Descartes, Newton and others. The idea of a relational, participatory view of the self and the world is both ancient and supported by contemporary fields of inquiry that feed into environmental thought; these include: general systems theory, quantum physics, the biological understanding of ecology, gestalt theory, field theory and so many more. The table below introduces key concepts of the participatory worldview by contrasting it with the dominant aspects of the current mechanistic worldview:[19]

Mechanistic Worldview	Participatory Worldview
Emphasizes reductionism	Emphasizes holism
Dualistic, subject—object approach to reality	Interactive, cooperative approach to reality
Ethically neutral and detached	Incorporates a strong axiological component
Universe is made of dead inert matter	Universe is active, animated and co-creative
Objects are external to the mind	General qualities of *sharing*, of *partaking* and of *interacting* exist at all levels of reality
Quantitative analysis	Qualitative analysis
Scientific method	Methodologies of participation and action research

As a philosophical perspective on the nature of reality, participation is an evolving worldview with broad and complex origins, including both long and deep roots in the Western philosophical canon (especially Romanticism) and more recent influences issuing from continental philosophy and the scientific community. Kenyan philosopher John Mbiti provides an excellent encapsulation of the participatory worldview, which closely resembles the idea from Thomas Berry mentioned earlier in the chapter. Mbiti captures the essence of a participatory worldview in his transformation of Descartes's famous dictum from, "I think therefore I am," to "I belong therefore I am" (Moodie 2004, 4).[20] Though this comment is made in reference to indigenous knowledge as it differs from imperialist systems of knowledge, and though it refers to belonging in a social sense, "I belong therefore I am" works just as effectively to describe the participatory view that all of life is interconnected.

The participatory reorientation toward belonging on a cosmic scale arises from the profound need to heal and replace the mind-body split deepened and systemized by Cartesian first philosophy. "I belong therefore I am" encapsulates the participatory expansion of human belonging from the level of human social communities and motivations to concern for the Earth and cosmic communities. This expansive, relational worldview transforms the schema for understanding the nature of the self in Western culture, offering new pathways for experiencing ourselves and the world.

Joanna Macy and Deep Ecology

I owe much of my orientation in deep ecology to the work of Joanna Macy. Macy's thinking contributes to an evolving ecological/relational/participatory worldview in a unique way. Her ideas derive from her blend of insights from East and West and converge with her inspiration by influential participatory thinkers such as Gregory Bateson. Inseparable from these influences are Macy's decades of political activism, and the impact of this work on the framing of her enquiry. Macy is in a circle of mutual influence in her work with Arne Naess (the Norwegian philosopher who coined the term *deep ecology*), and rainforest activists John Seed and Pat Fleming (*Thinking Like a Mountain: Towards A Council of All Beings* 1988). Important contributors to Macy's deep ecological vision include Ervin Laszlo's *The Systems View of the World: A Holistic Vision for Our Time* (1996) and Ludwig von Bertalanffy's foundational text, *General System Theory: Foundations, Development, Applications* (1968).

Deep ecologists call the relational wisdom of our connection with life on Earth the ecological self. This is one manifestation of what can also be called a model for the relational or participatory self. Arne Naess first introduced the concept of the ecological self as an extension of identification that goes beyond the experience of the ego self. In *Is It Painful to Think?: Conversations with Arne Naess,* with David Rothenberg,[21] Naess describes the usual cleavage thought to exist between the ego self and the surrounding self. He does not accept this separation, instead presenting a concept of the human ego that is enlarged and deepened beyond traditional Western standards.

In her book *World as Lover, World as Self*,[22] in the chapter "The Greening of the Self" Macy outlines why this wider, more relational metaphor of self is currently coming to the fore. The three conditions for the emergence of this ecological self, as she calls it, are: the breakdown of the conventional self by the spiritual and psychological impact of the destruction of nature; the offering by contemporary science of an alternative to the concept of a self that is separate from the world; and the upsurge of interest in non-dualistic spirituality, such as many find in Buddhism. As the subject/object separation loses theoretical and practical viability, the underpinnings of this belief in separateness are replaced by discoveries in twentieth-century science. These ideas suggest that no separation of self from an objective, outside world is possible. As just one example, Macy cites Heisenberg's uncertainty principle, which demonstrates that, at the level of the quantum, "the very act of observation changes what is observed."[23] Macy suggests that the systems sciences challenge long-held assumptions about the separate self. She shows that there is no logical or scientific evidence supporting the arbitrary separation of experience into one part that is "me," and everything else that is "other."

Quoting Naess in *Coming Back to Life*,[24] Macy refers to the wider sense of identity of the ecological self, seeing it as involving a natural maturation process: "We underestimate ourselves when we identify with the narrow, competitive ego."[25] With the development of the ecological self, we move to "a social self and a metaphysical self, but an ecological self as well."[26] Inspired by Gregory Bateson, Macy calls the ego self a "false reification." She contends that a separate self cannot be delimited. Instead, in systems language, each self is a flow-through of information. In Macy's words:

> *What I am, as systems theorists have helped me see, is a "flow-through." I am a flow-through of matter, energy, and information, which is transformed in turn by my own experiences and intentions.*[27]

Spiritual Ecology

The field of spiritual ecology in closely intertwined with deep ecology and participatory thought. Trying to capture the field of spiritual ecology in a few paragraphs is a difficult task. Not only has it been the focus of my study, teaching and work for more than half of my life, it is also the story of my unfolding spiritual experience and understanding of the world. What I offer here is a very small piece of a large and complex puzzle. My intention is to offer the beginning of a map for those who are new to this path and may wish to explore and expand their journey.

Spiritual ecology, also referred to as religion and ecology, ecojustice and sustainability and spirituality, inspires and chronicles the global religious responses to the immense environmental challenges of our era. The field touches on a broad range of contemporary theological, religious and spiritual themes in relation to the development of environmental thought. Spiritual ecological thinkers often engage with the interreligious reality of our world, and the need to cooperate and learn from each tradition. Spiritual ecologists encourage honoring and relating with the Earth community experientially through ritual. They often encourage the integration of Earth-based spirituality, from their own or other traditions, into more traditional Western religious practices and leadership.

While spiritual ecology is a diverse field covering a wide variety of perspectives, a commonality is revering all of life as sacred. Individual practitioners who describe themselves as spiritual ecologists often dip deeply into indigenous spiritualities and worldviews to support their work. Other streams of environmental thought inform spiritual ecology, such as ecotheology, environmental justice and ecofeminism.

Ecotheology is a form of spiritual ecology that focuses on the interrelationships of religion and nature, and particularly on environmental ethics. Ecotheology assumes that a relationship exists between human religious/spiritual worldviews and the choice between degradation or care for nature. Pope Francis' encyclical on the environment and human ecology, *Laudato Si* (2015), is probably the most influential piece of ecotheology ever written. *Laudato Si* has reached more people on the planet than any other work on environmental ethics and religion to date, shifting global consciousness on climate change, and influencing world leaders to create and ratify the Paris Climate Agreement seven months after its publication. Although responses to the Pope's encyclical varied greatly throughout the world, politicians and world leaders were unable to ignore the great swell of public support for his call for care for the Earth to take center stage as an essential moral and religious calling of humankind.

The Pope's call to action in *Laudato Si* also fits squarely with another field in spiritual ecology: environmental justice (also called ecojustice). Environmental justice is made up of grass-roots environmental activism by usually minority communities. These communities tend to be the ones that are disproportionately targeted with toxic waste and environmental hazards. Often, these movements intersect with spiritual ecological perspectives, and are bolstered through the organization and outreach of the religious organizations of threatened communities.

Paul Hawken, a well-known environmental thinker and author, began collecting names of groups working for social and ecological justice in the late 1990s. Astounded by the vast number of groups he discovered, he started a non-profit organization, WiserEarth.org, dedicated to collecting and connecting these many organizations. By his count, in 2009 there were at least two million groups working for social and environmental justice in communities around the world. Hawken describes this vast network of social action as expressing "humanity's collective genius, and the unstoppable movement to reimagine our relationship to the environment and one another."[28]

Ecofeminism is another important branch of spiritual ecology, and many books exist on the subject. Ecofeminism branches across disciplines to intersect with environmental justice, particularly through the work of physicist and environmental activist Vandana Shiva. Philosophically, ecofeminism compares the oppression of nature to the oppression of women and other "others." Spiritually, ecofeminism is often expressed through goddess and Gaia spirituality. Susan Griffin is an early and essential voice of ecofeminism. This quotation from her now-famous book, *Woman and Nature: The Roaring Inside Her*,[29] captures the awe and reverence for Earth often present in the environmental literature, and the shift toward Earth-consciousness that is central to deep ecology, the next section of this chapter:

He says that woman speaks with nature. That she hears voices from under the earth. That wind blows in her ears and trees whisper to her. That the dead sing through her mouth and the cries of infants are clear to her. But for him this dialogue is over. He says he is not part of this world, that he was set on this world as a stranger. He sets himself apart from woman and nature.[30]

Ecopsychology

The field of ecopsychology integrates the central tenets of visionary environmental thought, yet goes further by providing practical ways for moving toward the transformation described in this body of literature. The central idea of ecopsychology is that our psycho-spiritual health is dependent not only on healthy functioning within our human families and communities, but also on our healthy relationship with the more-than-human world. Disconnection from nature leads to much of the dis-ease that we experience: depression, anxiety and a sense that there is no meaning in life. Further, the dominant mechanistic-industrial worldview suggests to us that we live in a "dead" universe, devoid of meaning and magic.

Many of these "modern" ills can be traced back to the Western tendency to physically and conceptually separate ourselves from nature. We evolved to live outdoors, embedded in nature; now we spend most of our time indoors. The goal of ecopsychology practices in general is to heal the human/Earth split. This healing takes places by fostering awareness of ourselves in an ecological context. These approaches can inform the development of ethical shifts, psychological healing or spiritual transformation.

As a broad field, ecopsychology integrates environmental philosophy, spiritual ecology, indigenous knowledges, ecology and systems theory. Ecopsychology looks at our current attitudes toward nature as pathological. In his book *Green Psychology*,[31] Ralph Metzner describes psychopathological metaphors for the "destructive and exploitative behavior of the human species toward the natural world…"[32] Metzner argues that the first person to create such a metaphor was Paul Shepard, in his book *Nature and Madness*.[33] Shepard identifies the emergence of agriculture and the domestication of ourselves and other animals, 12,000 years ago, as the time that humans began to move away from the earth-connecting practices that functioned healthily for our species for over 100,000 years. This was the point at which humans began breaking away from a psychologically and ecologically healthy relationship with the Earth community. Metzner quotes Shepard as saying: "By aggravating the tensions of separation from the mother and at the same time spatially isolating the individual from the non-humanized world, agriculture made it difficult for the developing person to approach the issues around which the crucial passage into fully mature adult life had been structured in the course of human existence."[34]

While ecopsychologists generally acknowledge a sickness caused by disengagement from our true embeddedness in nature, they understand it as a condition which can be remedied. Not to return to a pre-civilized "state of nature," but to reintegrate an embodied Earth-honoring ethic of care into communities and civilizations across the globe. Many things need to happen politically, culturally and economically to create and represent this shift. The most essential ingredient needed to bring our global civilization into balance with Earth systems is to understand ourselves ecologically by integrating the reality that everything is connected.

From Environmental Theory to Earth-Connecting Practices

My approach to ecopsychology, and ecotherapy, centers on developing mindfulness of our interconnection with all of life. We know from the prolific work of many authors and practitioners, including a large body of quantitative research, that mindfulness heals. We know intuitively, and through a growing body of studies, that time in nature heals. Through combining environmental thought with mindfulness and other spiritual practices, we can learn to focus and to become present to the everything of which we are a part. The ecological self of deep ecologists, the wild self of ecofeminists, the ethic of care for the Earth of environmental philosophers or the relational self of participatory thinkers: all these notions of experience support expanding our sense of self through self-development.

My own brand of ecopsychology weaves the threads of environmental thought into practices that can re-indigenize Western minds. The following chapters embed my eco-spiritual processes within the broader context of environmental thought. I utilize mindfulness, through meditation and ritual, to bring the thinking of visionary environmental thought into the realm of experience. Sensitivity to our connections with Earth systems is the underpinning of an ethical relationship with Earth. The psycho-spiritual orientation that grows with the development of our Earth senses can impact individual and group actions at every level. By learning to honor the Earth as sacred, we come to feel in our bones that we are part of something greater than ourselves. Thus, living into the idea that everything is connected becomes a way of life that can fundamentally alter the underpinning belief structures of Western civilization.

Part 2

Earth-Connecting Practices

4

Earth-Connecting: The First Step of Earth Spirit Dreaming

This chapter begins the journey into the Earth-connecting step of the Earth Spirit Dreaming method. Developing Earth-connected consciousness — our perceptual connection with the web of the life-world — is essential to a re-indigenized spiritual awakening. Of course, we are connected with the life-world all of the time. Often, however, this connection is invisible to us. It exists as an unconscious attribute of our lives, albeit completely essential. I use the word "ecomindfulness" to describe my approach to developing Earth-connected consciousness. Ecomindfulness is a spiritual path that blends mindfulness practices with spiritual ecology to enhance embodied Earth sensitivities. Ecomindfulness begins the progressive consciousness shift of Earth Spirit Dreaming by suggesting simple ways to establish an embodied connection with the life-world. While connecting consciously with the life-world seems simple, it can be surprisingly challenging to slow down enough to find our way back to our natural senses.

Transforming Sustenance

One step toward developing full, Earth-connected embodiment is to learn to become conscious of our ecology: To become aware in an embodied way that we are interconnected with all of the life systems of the planet. We can know theoretically that we depend upon and impact the life systems of the planet, from the very big, the atmosphere (think climate change) to the seemingly more local, the water we drink and the air we breathe, the food we eat and the trees, dirt, plants and animals that are part of our community. However, knowing in our heads that we are integrated with our ecology (it could not be any other way), and experiencing/perceiving this reality are two different things. Without the fulfillment, meaning and energy that a conscious connection with life systems brings, it is challenging and maybe impossible to transition from a culture of consumption to one of connection with the Earth.

Many people in the West live in denial of our ecological terrain. Though there is a shift toward understanding the Earth as a network of integrated systems, as a biosphere, we still largely imagine that we are individual selves moving through the world relatively autonomously. This illusion of separateness is the source of many of our ills, both personally and collectively. German explorer Alexander von Humboldt, a central figure in originating the concept of ecology in the nineteenth century, realized that organisms could only be understood in the context of their environment. Understanding things by separating them out as individual parts or objects began to crumble in the face of the emerging understanding of ecology throughout the 1800s and 1900s. In the twenty-first century, in order to bring our lives back into balance with the Earth, it is time to integrate the reality of ecology on a psycho-spiritual level. This is a process that has been well under way as a stream of environmental thought since Ralph Waldo Emerson, and the American transcendentalists. Yet, after almost a century, the Western sense of self is stubbornly perpetuated and perceived as separate, individual and relatively self-sustaining.

The field of ecopsychology, which emerged in environmental thought in the 1980s and 90s, articulated in the terms of Western psychology that just as separation from and unhealthy relationships with the human community make us sick, so too do our separation from and unhealthy relationship with the natural. While these ideas already existed among some environmental activists, and in visionary environmental thought, it was Theodore Roszak, in his book *The Voice of the Earth*[36], who came up with a way to weave these ideas into a format and potential for practice that a broader audience, healing practitioners and therapists in particular, could relate to and act upon.

Roszak's dedication in the front of the book hints at an important influence in his life and work. He dedicates his book to Betty Roszak, quoting her essay "Rescue and Restore."[37] He thanks her for opening his eyes to the depth of Earth-connection emerging in Western experience and honors her for "awakening" him. Pointing out that she helped him "hear the voice" — hence the title of his book — he gets to the core of what was rising up as a global consciousness within the dominant Western culture then, and is continuing to rise up now. This wave of an alternative to industrial models of global society continues to stretch across the planet: a new stream of Earth-care, culture, story and values. Betty Roszak eloquently captures this spreading Earth-consciousness in her poem:

> ....*green voices are singing*
> *the dark ecstatic metabolism of hidden Earth.*
> *We may read the shaman's gestures,*
> *We bear the heat of eggs in our bodies,*
> *The clustering amorous atoms, molecules,*
> *Miracle of future flesh, magnificence of bone,*
> *arteries, sinew, spangled galaxies*
> *craving form.*[38]

We are coming to understand that what happens to the Earth affects us, and that we can impact Earth systems — life as we know it — more than, in previous eras, we ever imagined possible. To integrate this knowledge, we need to make the shift from experiencing Earth and her systems as something "out there," that we use to our own benefit. Part of dreaming a healing dream for the Earth is coming to know Earth as part of ourselves and, more importantly, ourselves as part of the Earth community. In Aldo Leopold's words, the shift to an "ethic for the land" requires that we see ourselves as citizens of the biotic community rather than its conquerors.[39]

When we make the shift to knowing in our bodies that we are interconnected with all of life, our primary psycho-spiritual sustenance transitions from consumption of the Earth to connection with the Earth. By sustenance I mean the beliefs, mores and community and personal experiences that provide us with life, meaning, purpose and a sense of belonging. Currently, our sustenance — what nourishes us physically, emotionally, spiritually — is most often derived from a dominant global culture that is unconnected from the Earth community. Shifting to sustenance that is more in balance with Earth systems underlies and empowers Earth-connected attitudes and ethics by providing alternatives for meaning, belonging and connection that are based on regenerative socio-political economies, social justice and human rights, and honoring Earth communities as sacred and intrinsically valuable. As we come to find our fulfillment and connection through connection with Earth systems, and our communities grow to define meaning, status, belonging and well-being in the context of connection rather than a model of use and consumption, we develop the emotional and spiritual ground necessary to transition to an Earth-honoring global civilization.

Developing Earth-Connected Consciousness

Consciousness is a complex idea and a complex experience that is difficult to capture in words. There are many definitions of consciousness, of how and why it's possible, or if it is possible at all. There is too much to say about consciousness to deal with it in this book in the depth that it deserves. The debates and questions surrounding "consciousness," which require the study of millennia-worth of ideas in metaphysics, epistemology and ontology from many cultures, are addressed in many books. For this discussion, we are going to assume that there is something called consciousness, and that, at least in some ways, we can change and focus our consciousness. For the Earth Spirit Dreaming method, I understand consciousness as something that evolves, and I make an educated and considered assumption that we can take part in and support this evolution.

Consciousness is both what we perceive and experience, and how our attention to the world and preconceived notions set the stage for these perceptions and experiences. Intertwined with this is the part of us that is physically and psychically connected with the world. At the same time, we are "the watcher": Able to watch the world while watching ourselves watching. To develop Earth-connected, or ecological, consciousness we move beyond the perceptual limitations of the human-created level of the world that is foremost in most of our minds and experience in Western culture. We expand our sense of self and awareness to include the realm of the life-world: A level of knowing that emanates from parts of our bodies and brains that are subconscious most of the time.[40]

To simplify the idea of discussing consciousness, I think of consciousness as a radio station: I can tune in to certain "stations" by how I think, act, take care of my body, engage in spiritual practice and community, and in the many other ways that I choose to live my life. There are many outside influences that inform and affect my consciousness "wavelength," which I can deal with in different ways. Sometimes another "station" will cross my signal of consciousness — a road rage driver for example. Or my husband will come home in a bad mood, and I will absorb and begin to reflect his mood. I can choose to let my consciousness drift to another "station," or signal, or I can work to maintain my own wavelength.

We are always embedded in a community of wavelengths of the human, and more-than-human, worlds. So, it can feel like a full-time job to steer through the web of wavelengths consciously. As I will discuss in more detail later in the book, we are either sending or receiving. We are either actively tuning our consciousness to our "station" of choice, or we are picking up and unconsciously vibrating to whatever other "stations" we encounter, often the loud, bright and shiny vibrations of our techno-industrial realm of life. Actively staying tuned in to and transmitting a spiritually awake, ecological consciousness, or any signal that we value, requires tremendous vigilance; the kind of vigilance that is developed through long spiritual practice; the kind of vigilance that can change the world.

While it is overwhelming to think about this level of responsibility, this is what is required to shift the very large entity that is our global civilization from a stream of destruction to a path of healing, light and life. Many people across the planet are working on this shift to a healing planetary consciousness in so many ways, and so much is already changing. It takes each one of us adding our own commitment and voice to this challenge of transforming global consciousness to make it a reality. And, it takes place in small moments, put together one after the other; many very simple, yet challenging, steps of conscious choices in each moment create a new path, a new culture, a new world.

As an example of the kind of small shifts in consciousness that are required, this morning as I walked my kids out to the car on the way to school, I noticed that a flock of birds were singing noisily and enchantingly from a tree in front of our house. Plenty of mornings I am too tired, frazzled and focused on the tasks at hand to notice these same birds. Today, by some grace, I stopped (though we were a little late) and said to my kids, "Listen to the birds." We all stopped our rush to the car (actually my rush, as they are more inclined to stop and listen to the birds). We had a moment of noticing the birds with our ears and eyes, to feeling their songs with our hearts, which led to noticing the late sunrise of the early fall sky. My personal and professional work are about being mindful of the life-world. So, maybe because of my commitment to this work, I was able to stop the rush to slip into this other mode of consciousness. However, many days it is challenging to remember to notice that I am connected with life all around me. This ability to be connected in this reality grows with time and practice, and I require continual reminders. In these and similar small ways, I try to expand my daily engagement in ecological consciousness, as well as the engagement of my students and clients. The practices and rituals that I will share in the next few chapters support the development of ecological consciousness, so that these moments of connection with life happen more often and for longer periods of time.

In order to cultivate ecological consciousness, I find I have to be very diligent quite often about creating moments of reflection, small and large. There are many articles and books available about how terrible our smartphones are, our social networking, our technology. I actually like these modes of being and find them creative and connective. And, I also find that they are entrancing; they are loud, bright, insistent, and constantly pull on our consciousness dial to the point that it can be hard to find time to develop and maintain other modes of consciousness that are primary modes of being when we are children. As I have rituals of checking my email, my texts, my phone, supported by beeps and bings throughout the day, I try to set up markers to remind me to tune in to ecological consciousness: to notice my connection with the life-world.

Connecting with the Life-World with Reverence

Ecological consciousness, as an idea and a way of being, is intertwined with the relationship of Westerners to indigenous people throughout the world. Ecological consciousness is a pathway back to our own connection to the land and our place within the web of life. In the company of some other thinkers and practitioners, I think of this as a returning for Western people.

The influence of indigenous culture on Western environmental thought is a faint trail that can be found with diligent detective work. Many paths of awakening to Earth-consciousness in Western thought can be traced back to contact with indigenous people. Two examples include Ralph Waldo Emerson's contact, and that of other transcendental thinkers, with Native Americans in the early 1800s. Another example is Aldo Leopold's interaction with Native Americans in the American southwest before and during his conception and writing of "The Land Ethic," a chapter from his *A Sand County Almanac* that is central to the development of Western environmental thought.[41]

Also, too often unremarked in environmental thought, but essential to a growing sense of the necessity of psycho-spiritual experience for creating a sustainable civilization, is the intersection of the ecofeminist and women's spirituality movements in opening doors to re-indigenized experience for Western people. These thinkers call out the patriarchal subjugation and oppression of nature and women (and other "others") as primarily responsible for the separation from and degradation of nature.[42]

And so, thus seen, we come to the juncture in the history of Western people where it is essential to come back to our connection with nature, with every aspect of our culture and belief structures, to rescue humanity from extinction and the Earth and other species from irreparable harm. Through an ethic of care for each other and the Earth — informing our actions from a perspective quite different than the one that got us to where we are now and reawakening our sensual belonging to life — we find our way into what feels new but what our bodies are born with. This "something deeper" is outside of the confines and accepted ways of knowing of the culture of the "rational." It is a sensual intensity of feeling our bodies as part of the Earth. In the context of ecological consciousness, living becomes a sacrament. As we do this work we are returning to and maturing back into the child's view of the world that we were born with. We enter an initiation into adulthood as citizens of the Earth community; we discover the truth of our responsibility to all of life and our co-creative abilities in dreaming the collective dream of the Earth.

Alongside the weight of responsibility, a feeling of the joy of living begins to seep in as we find our way back into alignment with a reverential, and decidedly non-linear, relationship with life.

We Are Always Connected

So how do we begin the journey back to our embodied relationship with the Earth? There are many simple ways to start connecting consciously with the life-world. Of course, we are connected all the time, but it's easy for this connection, essential as it is, to become a background, unconscious attribute of our lives. Like our hearts beating, or the ongoing rhythm of our breath, the life-world supports us and is the canvas of our lives. Despite the nature of our connection with the life-world, it is easy to forget this connection and to take it for granted. When we stop to notice our heart beating, it can be a surprising reminder of the miracle and fragility of our lives. In the same way, remembering the life-world in conscious ways can remind us of the complex miracle of life and, like our heartbeat, that we could not live without these systems. This awareness of the life-world is the underlying experience that leads to a sacred reverence for life on Earth. Yet, how do we start when so many of us feel too often so alone, and separate, in charting the course of our lives?

In a recent class, our discussion somehow led to the ways in which individual students experience themselves. They described feeling "on their own," taking care of themselves and feeling completely separate from everyone around them. This radical individualism underscores the American experience, and many ethical positions of American society, but, as I pointed out, my students are not at all on their own. Their beliefs are handed down to them and shared, their food is grown by others and cooked by others in the cafeteria, their cars and clothing and other "stuff" is made by others, their breathing, eating, sleeping, existing is made possible thanks to the trees and plants all around us. The atmosphere is made possible thanks to our place in the solar system and the daily incoming rays of the sun. Water comes from the complex, interworking systems of the planet. Endless complex systems of cells and organisms keep our bodies functioning, our food digesting, our lives running. We are not individuals, yet we seem perpetually trapped in this feeling.

Initially, my students were upset to think they were not individuals — although, perhaps in contradiction to this, at the same time they fear being on their own. I put forth a radical idea that they struggled to accept: It is an incredible gift that we are *not* on our own, but part of an intricate web of relationship in every moment of our lives. The existential loneliness we so often feel can be soothed by consciously rejoining the Earth community we are a part of in every moment of our lives and even after our deaths. *We are not alone.*

We can know and experience in every fiber of our being that we are not alone. However, only the intelligences of the Earth and Spirit realms can communicate this truth to us on the level that we need in order to see who we really are in relation with the cosmos. We come to know our relevance and importance, while also realizing that any individual is not so important. Hopefully, we are humbled by the vast reaches of knowing and being, the incredible "consciousnesses" that we encounter. Coming fully into our own nature as humans, we begin to learn our responsibilities as creators and dreamers, as care-takers and relatives of all beings. We discover how to meet at the boundary with the great mysteries and truths of life. Yet, we cannot get there with our rational minds; only our hearts and love, and a willingness to embrace the deepest feelings and mysteries of life, can guide us into awakened dreaming.

One day, recently, before a blood moon eclipse, I was driving up the narrow lane to my house when I noticed twenty or more turkey vultures resting on the fence by the side of the road and spread throughout the field. "Well, something died or is dying," I thought. I pulled my car over to commune with the visitors. The next morning, during my drumming, dancing and meditation time, I became curious about those vultures, the small condor species that peppers Ohio. What wisdom could I learn from them? What could their Latin name, *Cathartes aura*, illuminate for me; what belief or attachments could I let die; what could I let dry up and be transmuted into new energies in my life. I decided to create a ceremony to journey to the vulture spirit. I set my intention, raised my vibrations through rattling and meditations and leaned back into my soul light to step into the void.

I am walking along the ocean on a long, open beach. I know right away that I am on the California coast, walking along the Pacific Ocean, but in a time that I do not know, far back or forward. The ocean is huge and pulsing, reaching out to me with each wave. I feel the depth of the power of the ocean reach into my soul, feeding me the truth of her rhythms. I walk along the beach for quite some time, each step sinking into the wet sand, which sucks around my bare feet. The wind and noises of the beach surround me; gulls sing and whistle to one another, "There are the fish, over there."

Eventually, I come to an outcropping of dark stones typical of the northern California beaches. On these stones, a group of California condors perch, larger than life, larger than ever in this realm. I step up to the first and largest bird and ask: What is your wisdom? The wild, ancient spirit of condor blows into my spirit body, free and open, enchanting, beyond my understanding. Our minds struggle to meet in a place where we can share. After a time of watching, waiting and opening to the imprint of this bird, these words come to me: You are never alone. Such seemingly simple words for this penetrating exchange. They seem not enough, and yet this gift enters me fully, releasing a long pain, an ancestral grief in my family, in the structure of my species. I thank the condor and carefully retrace my steps to my portal into this world; returning slowly, carefully, completely I ground into my body and eventually to the quiet of my bedroom.

For the next weeks, I feel an effervescence of Earth community infiltrating my previously ingrained experience, filling a hole that I didn't realize was so long and wide, re-enchanting me into the music of the wild. I know the elemental energy of all of the friends and relations that surround me, know me, care for me: The birds landing on my porch, flying all around, singing, chirping, calling, the trees breathing air to me, the constant love and companionship of my dog, the huge-hearted softness of the horses grazing the field just beyond my front porch. The animal world, nature world, people world, spirit world always around me become newly lit up with some kind of love that I've forgotten, a feeling from long, long ago. I know now in a way that this body never fathomed and I say to everyone that will listen: We are never alone.

∼

We have not yet come to shamanic practice. That will come later in the book. But I tell this story now because it is one of the greatest gifts of my life to feel so intimately and acutely that we are surrounded always by rich and caring community on so many levels. My walks into other realms came after decades of sitting quietly in the woods. Still, I must do the beginning work each day to maintain my connection with Earth and Spirit in order to find my way into these realms again and again. Each time, I am starting over, creating the steps that take me from techno-industrial consciousness into Earth-consciousness. The next chapters offer practices to begin, or to continue, a path of initiation into adulthood as re-indigenized citizens of a community of story-makers, and into a tribal way of Earth-consciousness, as knowers, lovers and healers of life, in a planetary age.

5

Coming to Our Senses:
Slowing Down, Tuning In, Waking Up

We are now ready to lay the groundwork for Earth Spirit Dreaming. We begin by creating time and space in life for quiet and connection with ourselves, the instrument for finding our way back to life. I will emphasize again that while some of these early practices in the process seem simple, it becomes the recurring challenge of a lifetime to slow down under a ubiquitous pressure to produce. This chapter provides simple methods to begin waking up to ourselves, our bodies, our feelings and our experience. Readers are encouraged to begin these practices by finding small moments to allow different kinds of sensitivities to open in our bodies: to slow down and connect with ourselves and nature. These simple, and challenging, practices are activities that were a large part of everyday life for the majority of human existence. While quiet moments to really feel life all around us are now in short supply, our body-heart-minds respond with such joy and relief when we do find these moments, as if we are coming home to something so often just out of reach.

Earth sensitivities are quiet and soft compared to many common forms of engagement. Slowing down is required to allow these sensitivities forward. The sensory intensity of contemporary Western culture quells the softer sensations of Earth-connection. Larger percentages of the human race live in cities now than ever before. Many of us are also immersed in the dominant global culture on the Internet. This shift in demographics and culture means that many of us are often surrounded by crowds, traffic, news feeds, advertisements and unprecedented amounts of entertainment at our fingertips. Slowing down in these highly overstimulating conditions takes practice and commitment, yet offers opportunities for profound changes in our perception of ourselves and the world.

Doing Nothing

Doing nothing is an essential fuel for many of the best parts of human nature: creativity, moments of awe, heightened intuitive capabilities, learning, integration, flashes of brilliance and profound shifts in consciousness. If it is hard to imagine slowing down your productive life to do nothing, remember that the results can be astonishing. Energy and insight can soar from a regular commitment to resting and "doing nothing." To intensify the effect, do nothing for longer periods. To make it even more effective, do nothing while sitting in nature. If you sit long enough outside, doing nothing, this is called a vision quest.

Over time, I have noticed that the harder it feels to slow down directly correlates with our need to do nothing. If you feel you are absolutely too busy to do nothing, then you are most in need of doing nothing. When our activities feel so pressing that we can't conceive of slowing down, that is a sign that we have lost contact with our "flow," the aspect of ourselves that is our primal wisdom and connection. I am a person who loves to be busy! It is a central aspect of my life's work to learn to slow down. I often need reminding and encouragement to do it. We all do; we need to build the gift of slowing down into the fabric of habits that make up our communal spaces.

It is often in the cracks of life that the windows to other worlds seep in. When we are still, we notice the bright red bird outside the window, the wind blowing through the grass, the shapes of raindrops on our windshield. These are the moments that are to be sought after and cherished on our journey back to life. It does not mean that we need to get rid of technology, but we must foster our relationship with quiet and stillness as a first step to fostering Earth connected consciousness.

Cultivating Boredom

We are all so free from boredom now. With our phones — instant answers to almost any question, the chance to get one more thing done, return one more phone call, send that email — almost every moment can be filled. With the increase in technology, from which does also come great rewards, we have lost our access to boredom. Access to boredom? Surely boredom is boring, a bore, not something we want. But, like many things we struggle to understand and appreciate until they are gone, boredom has qualities that are imperative to our well-being. In terms of transforming our consciousness toward Earth and Spirit connection, boredom is a gateway experience. Often, when shifting from one mode of consciousness to another, there can be a period of anxiety, restlessness and boredom. Certainly, when "gearing down" from the high-speed overstimulation of techno-industrial consciousness — there is also mechanistic consciousness mixed in there — we are shifting from one kind of connection to another. While these names of cultural paradigms are just markers along the way — the map, not the territory — they are important as signposts for journeying across thresholds in our minds.

EXERCISE: Unstructured Time and Musing

Purpose

One way to slow down and get in touch with our own connectedness with the life-world is through unstructured time, the forerunner of musing. Or rather, good old-fashioned boredom. There are certain kinds of work that our brains and "beings" do when we are "bored," and when our minds are just wandering, that they don't do at any other time. Boredom and musing are the times when our brains build connections and links between our disparate experiences and create stories and meaning. Downtime is connection and creation time.

Description

To begin slowing down, make dates with yourself to do nothing for 15 minutes at a time. Try to create moments of quiet: leave your phone, computer and other tasks that are pulling on you in another room, and make sure that they are silenced completely. It is helpful to set an alarm on your phone or clock (left in another room) so that you don't have to check the time. Find a place to sit or lie down where you feel comfortable and relaxed, away from any work or chores that are pulling on you. If you can, find a window to look through, or gaze at a plant, a splash of natural light on the wall, or even a lovely piece of cloth or place in the room that seems attractive, orderly or beautiful to you. If you are able to, take this doing "nothing" time outside.

Commit to doing nothing for at least 15 minutes on a regular basis. Since challenges will come up at first, with both time and attitude, plan to make this commitment to doing nothing as easy as possible. It can be tempting to want to "achieve" results, but this is part of the "producing" consciousness that's caused this lack of quiet time to begin with. As you move out of the dominant consciousness of the surrounding culture, there will often be a kind of drag on you; you may feel a resistance to the shifts that you are seeking. Step through them and continue.

Whatever feels most doable is what will work. Once a week is better than once a day if you feel less stressed with this level of commitment. The platitude "less is more" is very useful when beginning to make space for moments of quiet and boredom. During this time, don't meditate, don't watch your breath, don't do yoga; as much as you can, allow yourself to make nothing happen. Achieve absolutely nothing. This is a time for complete cessation of all accomplishment, activity, achievement and productivity.

EXERCISE: Cultivating Ecological Consciousness
Purpose

Cultivating ecological consciousness begins with slowing down the pace of our lives, our minds and our bodies. We are programmed by the cultural beliefs and expectations of even our most intimate communities to exist in a state of producing to fit into the mores of current economic and social conventions. And yet we must move through the fears that arise when we step into other states of being if we are to find our way home to the genetic sensitivities that bring an authentic feel and experience of our ecology. Our natural context in the web of life is a real and touchable world. It can be hard to see how slowing down can encourage transformative changes of perception and, further, how these shifts in perception can bring humans and the planetary systems back into balance. The resistance that often arises can make slowing down even more complex and challenging. Also, many of us no longer know how to slow down, so we have to learn, with sometimes many antsy and anxiety-producing sessions leading up to the shifts that eventually occur. The natural world will support us through this process and the joy with which the Earth community responds to our return inspires more and more connection, joy, healing and, eventually, more attraction, to these moments of quiet reflection.

Description

There are many ways to practice ecological consciousness individually, within the activities and rituals already built into your life. Certainly, slowing down as described in the previous exercise is the first and best place to start. Also, if you already have a spiritual practice, you can find ways to build in your ecological consciousness practice within already established rituals. As a first step, if you take time to pray or meditate everyday, you can use part of this time to be thankful for the Earth systems that support your life, and the beings that share your immediate world. Ingraining deep feelings of gratitude for every natural phenomenon that you notice sets these everyday moments apart as sacred events, rather than the background of life that we often take for granted.

Once we are creating moments of quiet and reflection, and embodying the returning sensations that these moments provide, we are ready to re-tune in to nature through daily mindfulness practices. In the next chapter, I discuss different definitions of nature: human nature, nature as something "out there," separate and pristine, and nature as an evolutionary principle. We will be following exercises that move us toward connecting with nature as we typically think of the word, by spending time in natural settings.

6

Cultivating Ecomindfulness: Increasing Our Conscious Connection with Nature

Awakening natural senses, a seed of ecological consciousness, is best done, in the beginning, by becoming mindful of the natural world. Once we are awakened to nature in general, it becomes easier to maintain ecological consciousness without being in a "nature" setting such as the woods, a park or a yard. A reward of mindfulness in nature is often a deeper appreciation for our own natures, and the revelatory discovery that we are nature. We begin to see ourselves mirrored in nature, and nature mirrored in us. Reconnecting with the patterns and rhythms in nature helps illuminate our own recurring patterns.

No matter how or where we live, we are alive and functioning because we are always connected within our natural settings. After slowing down, we come to the practice of ecomindfulness: Intentionally and consistently tuning in to the natural world around us through daily mindfulness practices wherever we are. Mindfulness practices increase our state of being conscious, or aware of something. When we are developing ecomindfulness, we are using practices that help us become more aware of our connection with nature, and more specifically of our dependence on and connection with our ecology.

Nature in an ecological context requires broadening the most commonly held understanding of "nature," such as parks, woods, mountains and wilderness. Ecologically, the term "nature" encapsulates human nature, in the sense that we cannot exist or be understood outside of our role in our ecological context. "Nature" also stands for the entirety of the biosphere and our embedded relationship with this network of interwoven systems. With this complexity in mind, our work to reconnect with the life-world begins simply: by remembering to regularly notice the natural world.

When we cultivate mindfulness of the life-world, and our place in it, we shift from focusing on the world as objects to focusing on relationships and interconnection between beings and things. We come to hold as a daily aliveness — through study, contemplation and practice — our relationship with one another and with all of life on Earth. As we engage in this transformation of our self-perception, the felt experience of separateness begins to fall away. As we come to feel the depth of our intimate connection with all of life, our experiences and our actions begin to radically change.

As we begin to focus on relationships, we can awaken sensitivities that too often lie dormant. In his book *The Participatory Mind*, Henryk Skolimowski calls these sensitivities "participatory." As discussed in detail in Chapter Three, a participatory worldview assumes that the underlying fabric of reality is relationships.[43]

To perceive these relationships we begin to develop senses beyond the "five" that we in Western culture are used to thinking of and using.[44] Ecopsychologist Michael J. Cohen suggests that we have 54 natural senses. In his book *Reconnecting With Nature* he says:[45]

> *Often we are habitually conscious of the world through the following three senses:*
>
> *1. Sight*
> *2. Language*
> *3. Reason*
>
> *Our highly trained and educated three-sense perceptions often overpower our other awareness abilities. This leaves our consciousness and thinking devoid of our many other non-language, sensory ways of knowing and being.*
>
> *For this reason, it makes sense to produce some nature-connected moment in which we may thoughtfully discover and experience, first hand, many other natural ways of knowing that we inherit from nature.*[46]

The practice of ecomindfulness helps us notice our embeddedness in the life-world: The web of life systems that intersects with every aspect of our lives in any given moment.[47] Opening up to this reality transforms our sense of ourselves and helps us experience the individual self as a conceptual construction. As we deepen this practice through meditation in nature, this connection with something larger than ourselves opens a doorway to experience that we might think of as spiritual as our continuous encounter with the miracle of life brings us face to face with the mysteries of the cosmos.

Ecomindfulness Practices

Daily ecomindfulness can be supported through many kinds of practices. Traditional mindfulness methods that help us to tune in to our direct experience work very well. In order to cultivate ecomindfulness, it is easiest to create intentional nature-connecting rituals that fit easily in your normal schedule. The more that I incorporate ecomindfulness rituals into my daily routine, the more I notice the support of the life-world in absolutely every moment of my life. This is one way that I try to be mindful of my ecology on a daily basis.

Beyond becoming increasingly intentional about noticing nature throughout your day, any mindfulness practices that are done with a focus on nature will enhance natural sensitivities; interaction with nature through creativity and movement exercises done outdoors are good places to start. Through nature-focused exercises and rituals, ecological consciousness increases gradually over time, eventually completely transforming our perceptions and sense of self. These small changes in habit reorient us into increased balance with the Earth. Done in community, in webs of like-minded people that reach out and intersect with other Earth-focused communities, these small changes are growing into big shifts in planetary consciousness. This is happening now and has been for decades. This web of Earth-connection and healing is speeding up and expanding at unprecedented rates. Those of us who have been engaged in this practice over decades can feel the exponential increase of "shift" that is now upon us.

EXERCISE: Small Moments with Nature

Purpose

With this simple practice, our connection with all of life progresses day by day. As we connect with nature in small moments on a regular basis, our bodies begin to wake up to our embeddedness within our ecological community.

I try to be very diligent about creating moments of reflection outside. I build these moments into my daily routine in ways that become habitual. Every time I step outside, I try to take a moment to stop and take in the sights, smells and activity of nature all around me. I remind myself that every breath I take is courtesy of the biosphere. I stop to experience profound gratitude for the systems and beings on the planet that make my life possible. The more I do this, the more I notice the support of the life-world in every moment of my life.

Description

By noticing nature more and more, increased mindfulness of the ecological fabric of our lives can become self-perpetuating. To begin, find something that you often pass that can act as a trigger to notice nature. Set a subconscious reminder to galvanize this practice. Find something that is part of your regular landscape and tell yourself that every time you see this you will stop what you are doing and remember that you are part of the life-world. An example is to commit to do this every time you see a certain tree, or every time you see or hear a bird. During these moments, intentionally wake up your senses and feel this moment and the nature being that inspired it; allow yourself to become suffused with gratitude that your life is possible because of the combined life systems of the planet.

Another way to create daily mindfulness of your ecology is to choose a specific time each day when you take a moment to notice nature. Try to find a place in your daily routine to fit in a small moment to relate to nature. Make this ritual something that feels manageable within the framework of your life. I try to actively sense nature every time I walk from my house to my car.

Make a habit of touching nature when you can. When I notice something in nature, I often stop to gently touch it. I run my hands across my bushes on my way out of the door, I press my palm against the bark of the tree by my driveway, I pick up a small rock as I walk into my office and put it back when I leave.

Another possibility is to decide on a specific number of breaths that you will take to consciously immerse yourself in your ecological context during your small moments in nature. I know that no matter how busy I may be, I always have time for three breaths to be with the sight and sounds of the natural world. You have time, too, and these three breaths will add up to many breaths over days, and months, and years. The world's problems seem so big; it's hard to imagine that we can make changes in three breaths. But we can. The thought-shifting, the dream-changing, that we do in these small moments become part of a chain of ripples across the planet. Envision your three breaths, your small moments, blending with millions of other people's small moments across the Earth.

These moments matter, they grow and shift the story. To increase your understanding of the scope and magnitude of the communities all over the world that are creating change through the "small moments," see Paul Hawken's book *Blessed Unrest*. Together, we are growing a very large movement of Earth healers across the planet; each seed planted contributes to the very large and growing garden that is the origin and the result of an emerging healing dream of the Earth.

EXERCISE: Spending Time Outdoors Each Day
Purpose

While we spend most of our time inside, many of our ancestors spent most of their time outside. Time outside wakes up our senses and can be surprisingly restorative. Time in nature reduces stress, lowers our heart rate and blood pressure and encourages the development of healthy cells in our bodies. Scientific studies increasingly support what we know from intuition and experience: the beauty of the world is restorative. A long-term study conducted in Japan on forest bathing, or *shinrin-yoku*, concluded that time in nature boosts the immune system by increasing the development of "killer" cells that fight cancer and other diseases (Qing Li, et al., 2009).[48]

Description

Try to find a natural location that you can visit frequently. Many people, especially in cities, find it difficult to find natural settings where they feel safe and relaxed. Going in groups might be easier and more comfortable. If you live in a loud or unsafe place, or cannot get to a natural setting, create a space of nature in your house. A terrarium, a small garden of pots, vertical indoor gardens or a small window garden are excellent ways to create "nature" indoors. I often use rocks inside as well. If you cannot go out, commit to bringing nature in for a daily practice of connection. This prayer by 18th century rabbi Nachman of Bratzlav inspires me to commit to this important mindfulness practice:

> *Grant me the ability to be alone; may it be my custom to go outdoors each day, among the trees and grass, among all growing things, and there may I be alone, and enter into prayer, to talk with the One to whom I belong.*
>
> *May I express there everything in my heart, and may all the foliage of the field (all grasses, trees and plants) may they all awake at my coming, to send the powers of their life into the words of my prayer so that my prayer and speech are made whole through the life and spirit of all growing things.*[49]

EXERCISE: Walking Barefoot on the Ground
Purpose

The book *Earthing: The Most Important Health Discovery Ever!*, by Clinton Ober and Dr Stephen T. Sinatra M.D.,[50] discusses many studies that support the simple act of walking barefoot on the ground for health. The authors suggest that, at minimum, we should walk barefoot on the ground for 30 minutes a day. While I feel many positive effects from doing this, I find it hard to incorporate 30 minutes of barefoot walking into my life every day (especially in the colder months!).

I practice outdoor meditation at a medicine wheel that I have built in the woods, up the hill behind my house. As I sit, I enjoy watching two creeks tumble down small gorges to meet at the crumbling old stone railroad tunnel. After a bit of repulsion at the muddy ooze that I often find on the slippery hill between my backyard and the medicine wheel, I decided to walk barefoot to the wheel each time I go, affording me 20 minutes of barefoot time. I also meditate at the wheel barefoot, which can add minutes, and sometimes hours. My feet get muddy! My toenail polish chips! Sounds ridiculous, I know, but I think we need to dig out our resistances to walking barefoot on the Earth, which was a basic fact of human life for millennia. We evolved to walk barefoot on the Earth, and, like many basic biological realities before "civilization" and industrialization, these things turn out to be very important to our health and well-being, beyond what we know or can imagine within the framework of our current "science."

Description

There is not much in the way of instructions for walking barefoot on the ground. The real work is to explore whatever blocks we may have to this very basic human function. For some people, this is an easy and comfortable practice. For others, I've found that no amount of encouragement will get them to walk barefoot on the ground. Sometimes this can be for medical reasons or because of injuries. Often, I find that people have fears of nature or the woods, or of getting injured, that get in the way. Also, if we have our shoes on most of the time, it can be painful to begin walking barefoot. Another option is to sit with your hands on the Earth. Surprisingly, I often find people are more comfortable with this, especially if they can sit on a blanket or waterproof pad on the ground. Find whatever way is most comfortable for you to touch the Earth with your bare skin.

EXERCISE: A Grounding Meditation

(this meditation can be done with or without shoes)

Begin with your feet planted firmly on the ground, in a standing position. Slowly and deliberately, begin rolling your feet around on the ground so that every surface of your toes and feet make contact with the Earth at some point. It is okay to do this through your shoes but doing it barefoot is ideal.

Feel each part of your foot begin to wake up. Imagine breathing in and out through the bottom of your feet, feeling the energy of the Earth meeting the soles of your feet, and eventually your energy body. When breathing out, imagine that you are reaching with the breath from your body down to meet the interiors of the Earth, through levels of dirt, maybe aquifers, through layers of old and older rock to the searing heat of her molten heart. Imagine that you can feel the fullness and steady thrumming, the pulsing energy, of the Earth.

Imagine that there is one beat of the heart of the Earth for every breath that you take. Once you can clearly imagine that you are reaching down with roots to touch the inmost bass notes of the rhythm of the Earth, let that heavy thrumming move slowly up your body. Roll your ankles, move your knees, swing your hips slowly around in a circle, undulate your spine up and down, roll your shoulders, reach in large circles backward, and then forward, with your arms, roll your head sideways, forward and back, then in a circle. Once your body is awake, return again to the feeling of your body reaching down through your feet to touch the powerful beating of life. Send gratitude and love through each breath, say a prayer of gratitude for all the Earth does to allow you to exist and to support your learning in ways that intertwine with her dreams.

EXERCISE: Sitting or Lying on the Earth
Purpose

Recently, I went with a friend to do yoga in the woods. Just as perceptions in general are intensified in the woods, so is the experience of doing yoga. As I stood in Tree Pose, I found my vision aligned with a tree that came from the small creek gorge we were overlooking. The branches of the tree extended high into the sky. Just a few feet from this tree, slightly slanting on the edge of the hill, I found my relationship to my own balance intensified by the knowledge (really just fear) that if I lost my balance I might fall over the edge. At the end of my practice, I moved into Child's Pose, pressing my cheek against the loamy dirt and dry leaves. With my face and legs, and the backs of my arms and hands, pressed to the Earth, I felt connected and safe. Flipping over to lie flat on my back, I gazed at the sky through interlacing layers of green leaves as they whispered and moved in the wind.

Description

Like walking barefoot on the Earth, few directions are required for sitting or lying on the ground. The important thing to do is to find somewhere that is safe and as comfortable as possible. Going in groups helps the feeling and reality of safety, and truly expands this communal experience with nature. Use a blanket, a pad or a yoga mat if that is helpful. Wear old clothes that you don't mind getting dirty or wet. Many people are not comfortable lying face down, or even face up, on the bare ground. That is okay. Whatever works for you is the best way to do the practice.

The simple act of lying on the ground, one that children do naturally, fills me with such profound gratitude for something as basic, and as miraculous and beautiful, as leaves.

Thich Nhat Hanh offers guidance for lying on the Earth in his article, "I Want to Be Grounded," that he contributed to the magazine *Shambhala Sun* in July 2012.[51]

EXERCISE: Lying on the Earth, by Thich Nhat Hanh

You may like to lie on the Earth and be in touch with our beautiful planet. The Earth can receive all our pain and tension, and she gives us protection and energy. We know that countless cells in our body are constantly being born and dying. In every moment Mother Earth produces us as a wonderful manifestation and receives us back. When we die, we return to her, and she brings us forth again.

You might have a conversation with Mother Earth: "Dear Mother Earth, I am clearly aware that you are present in me and I am part of you. You gave birth to me and provided me with everything I needed for my nourishment. You give me air to breathe, water to drink, food to eat, and medicinal herbs to heal me when I am sick. Because you gave birth to me once, I know that you will continue to give birth to me again and again in the future. That is why I can never die. Each time I manifest, I am fresh and new. Each time I return, you receive and embrace me with great compassion. You are the great Earth, this beautiful blue planet."[52]

EXERCISE: Sitting or Lying Down with Rocks

Purpose

As an addition or alternative to lying outside on the ground, you can place rocks on your body while either sitting or lying down. Focusing on the feeling and pressure of the rocks is the practice. Rocks are very grounding. They are the oldest part of Earth surrounding us at any one time and, as I've learned by knowing and speaking with rocks, they hold the original dream of the planet, the earliest intention of the cosmic expression of life. Rocks hold and represent ancient history, and help us connect with old, old knowing. Memories of the past can arise during rock meditations, both the past of our own lives and ancestral memories buried deeply into our DNA. Holding the memory of the original intention of the Earth, rocks illuminate the spirit calling that brought each of us into form in this time and place.

Description

I collect rocks that I keep in my house and office. I ask and listen for guidance when seeking these rocks. I ask if they want to come into my life to share my journey for a while. To be with them, I simply lie on the floor, or on my bed, in a comfortable position. I place rocks onto my body wherever it feels good to do so. In a group, you can take turns placing rocks on each other's bodies, and listening as the person lying or sitting with rocks talks about what comes up for them. There can be laughing, tickling and often tears as we remember ourselves in both very old and very new ways. Be sensitive to individual comfort levels regarding touching bodies, and respect boundaries at all times.

Ask the person you are putting rocks on what areas of their body they are comfortable having you place rocks. Ask the rocks themselves for guidance; listen to your intuition; trust yourself when doing this very special practice, either for yourself or for others.

For this practice, you can use rocks that you collect outdoors, or that you buy from a store. Many people work with crystals in this way. I like crystals, but I mostly work with "regular" rocks I find in my yard, in the woods and in various places I go to. I have a bag of sacred rocks I take with me to work with in my personal practice, and when I work with others as a facilitator or guide. Everyone can foster a relationship with a set of sacred stones that they meet in reverence and get to know over time.

EXERCISE: Creating a Set of Sacred Stones
Purpose

If you live in the city, or travel often, one way to create a "natural setting" to carry with you is to find, and cultivate, your own set of sacred stones. Over time, you can build up a collection of intentionally activated sacred stones. These stones eventually become a basis for vibrational and shamanic work, which I will discuss later in this book. For now, begin to know and care for your own sacred stones; remember that they choose you as much as you choose them, and sometimes more so.

Description

To begin working with your set of stones, start with seven stones representing earth, air, fire, water, Spirit, cosmos and the veil to other realms.[53] To find your stones, go to a local creek or area in nature that feels beautiful to you, or visit a store or your own existing collection if you feel more drawn to work with crystals, either in general or at the current time. Sacred stones change and move, following their own flow and yours over time.

When you seek stones, ask the area or place that you are visiting if you may seek a stone to take with you. Feel with your body and your intuition for a response. If you get a good feeling, go ahead and collect your stones. If you get a bad or uncomfortable feeling, do not take a stone from that place. Gaze intently at any stone that attracts you. Ask the stone with your body and heart if it would be willing to leave with you to become a part of your set of sacred stones.

It is important to remember that we do not own the stones. They have their own inherent history and ends. Though stones do not have human experiences, we can use our own experience to attempt to relate to their wildness and individual stories. Yes, we are projecting our own kinds of perceptions onto the stones, but it is for a useful reason. Since we cannot be stones, we use our own experiences as humans to relate to them. Be ready to release them or return them to the Earth at any time, based on continually checking with your intuition about each stone. My stones sometimes seem to want to "re-Earth" by staying in the woods or taking some time in my creek. Over time, the stones can lose their Earth power, as they tend to ground us by taking on heavy energies. Re-Earthing your rocks helps them return to their natural vibrations. My set is currently in my medicine wheel after a hiatus in the creek by my house (where I sometimes cannot find them again). One of my rocks is a very powerful vision stone that I found on the beach of an island on Lake Erie. Another is a healing crystal to which I am very attached (note: at the time of this writing, both of these stones are now gone on their journeys to other people or places).

One of my absolute dearest stones holds the imprint of a 150-million-year-old fossil. I found it by a rock covered with petroglyphs carved by a tribe that lived in Ohio 4,500 years ago. While using this precious vision rock during a ceremony in a friend's backyard, I felt drawn to place the stone in her mandalas of stones and leave it there. It was hard to let go of that rock. Again, I am aware that I am anthropomorphizing the stones. I do it consciously in an attempt to relate to them. It is a method for increasing my sensitivity to their energy, movements and unfolding cycles of time and evolution.

As you bring stones home with you, take time to feel into their subtle energies. One way of doing this is to place the stone near your bed, or under your pillow, and set the intention to dream with the stone for a few nights, or even a week. While dreaming with the stone, you can discover archetypal and symbolic meanings that the stone can represent for you or draw into your life. Your set can be used in daily meditation, rituals and ceremony and during your outdoor spiritual practice. You can also use your sacred stones to build medicine wheels on your floor, table or altar. Be creative! I use a few sets of stone of various sizes, depending on where I might use them, and based on their weight and energetic imprint. I have a large basket of stones at home that is too heavy to carry, a medium-sized bag of stones for classes, retreats and workshops, and a small bag of especially sacred stones that I use in ceremonies and healing sessions. Let the stones become a part of your spiritual practices in unusual and creative ways; let the stones guide you.

Once we are more connected to our ecological context, and the nature beings all around us, we are ready to deepen our sense of place with the land where we live and visit. The practices in the next chapter focus on restoring a connection with patterns and cycles in nature that are often lost or overshadowed in the dominant Western worldview. Finding, and returning again and again, to the same place unlocks and supports our natural attunement to the rhythms of nature. Developing a relationship with a specific place over time helps us to feel more at home in the web of life, and to fulfill the very human need to feel integrated with specific natural settings.

7

Returning to the Land: Connecting with the Rhythms and Cycles of Nature

Finding a sense of place with the land restores a connection that is often lost or overshadowed. Finding a place, and returning to it again and again, unlocks our natural attunement to the cycles and rhythms of nature. Returning to a place that we develop a relationship with over time helps us to "re-Earth," to develop the very important human experience of a sense of place. Many of us living in techno-industrial cultures are wandering alone, devoid of a connection with the land. It is through the deeply inherited human sense of place that we realize that we are always connected, that we are never alone.

As we grow into relationship with a sacred place in nature, we can watch with eager excitement for the first buds of spring, the slanting morning sun of summer glistening on the dew, feel the first snowflakes of winter melt on our skin, allow the stunning colors of fall to pierce our hearts with their breathtaking intensity, lie among the earthy smell and texture of a pile of leaves. As with human friends and family, we come to know natural places over time with intricacy and love, questions and concerns, sometimes fear and frustration, and often with joy and the fulfillment found in the intimacy of the connection. Never perfect, always necessary, knowing and loving our place on Earth firmly informs our identity, often whether we know it or not.

Psychotherapist William Cahalan, in his article "Ecological Groundedness in Gestalt Therapy," offers a useful framework for understanding the enfolding of our self in relationship with the land.[54] The author focuses his discussion on groundedness, which he defines as "a dynamic state of the person that includes the sense of confidence, pleasure, and wonder resulting from progressively deepening contact with the wild and domesticated natural community of the person's neighborhood and larger land region..." He continues:

> *Being grounded is enhanced and renewed by periods of extended, sensuous, empathic engagement with the world, balanced by restorative moments of inward reflectiveness. This rhythm involves an intuitive cycling between the individual's more contracted, contained sense of self, on the one hand, and a more expanded, relational, or extended sense of self on the other, including the ability to lose oneself at times in union with the world. When we experience this self-extended state, the Earth tends to be sensed as the all-embracing, enduring Self of which the individual is one unique but temporary expression.[55]*

To be grounded, then, is not just an analogy for a feeling within ourselves. It is both a state of feeling in balance metaphorically, and a reality of really and truly being on the ground. Knowing the actual ground upon which we wake, sleep, wonder and walk through our lives each day is the basis for true "groundedness." The "ground," the phenomenological framework of our experience, is rooted in the ground — real, dirty, loamy, sandy, rocky, barren, fecund — beneath our feet. In this way, we move from concept to connection with our sense of place; our lives take on new balance as we literally return our focus to the feeling of the dirt beneath our feet, again, and again, and again.

EXERCISE: Find and Return to a Special Natural Place
Purpose

Making a ritual of returning to the same place helps us tune in to our natural sensitivity to change, cycles, patterns, the space and timing and the rhythms of nature. Nurturing a relationship with a special place opens atrophied channels of relatedness with all of life. Over time, we can come to truly and deeply love many places in nature. This practice draws more awareness to the ways in which we naturally come to love nature; our garden, the beach we visit again and again, special mountains, a green space in our town. Most of us already feel a connection with special places in nature. What is needed is to be more conscious of the profound importance of honoring and nurturing our relationship with these places.

Description

There are many ways to create a relationship with a special natural place. You can go to a nature area near your home, in the woods, in a park, or even in your backyard. Using your intuitive embodiment (gained through the quieting and grounding exercises from Chapter Six), ask yourself and the place if this is a good match for a long-term relationship. If you feel unsafe, or feel any kind of "bad energy" in the place, it is not a good place to relate to over time. These kinds of feelings can come from negative things that have happened in a place, or animals or other natural beings that aren't open to human contact. Feel in your body, place your feet directly on the ground, lightly touch your "gut," to tune in to your body knowledge. Take the time to find a place that feels good, open, energizing and special. In his book *Reconnecting With Nature*, Michael J. Cohen suggests the following approach when choosing a special place:

> Ask it if it will help you learn from it. It will not give consent if you are going to injure, destroy or defame it, or it you. Wait for about half a minute. Look for adverse signals of danger such as thorns, bees, cliff faces, etc. If the area still feels attractive, or becomes more attractive, you have gained its consent. If this portion of the natural area you visit no longer feels attractive, simply select another natural part that attracts you and repeat this process. Do this until you find an area where a safe attraction remains.[56]

If you don't have a place to go or can't get to a place that feels natural and safe, you can create a place indoors or on a porch. When creating a place indoors, go through the same procedure of using your intuition to direct you to a location in your home that feels attractive. It's important to create this space in a low-traffic area: this can be a room, a corner, a tabletop, or even a shelf. When you are outside, feel with your embodied intuition for an attraction to certain beings in nature to bring into your home or office to create your special nature place. Rock, leaves, sticks, pine cones all work well for this task. You can also create a small "nature area" in an indoor pot, or a terrarium. When creating your pot or terrarium allow a sense of sacred creativity to permeate finding the container(s), plants and dirt for your sacred indoor nature space. Collect small rocks, create a small pond with a bowl embedded in the dirt. Make a fairy wood. You can also plant a pot, or a few pots, with seeds and watch them grow over time as your sacred relational nature practice.

Gardens are a natural way to cultivate connection with your land, and create built-in rituals for returning again and again to the same place within the cycles of the seasons. Gardens are one of the most well-known and acceptable ways in Western culture to cultivate ecological consciousness. Growing and tending to gardens of any size, inside or out, deepens connection with the life-world. Eating the plants that we tend with love emphasizes the depth of interrelatedness with the web of life. Gardens give us an opportunity to connect with Earth in an embodied way through daily gardening tasks. When gardening, we use all of our senses; not only the five that we tend to think of, but other Earth sensitivities that help us relate to and cherish our plants.

Once you have chosen or created a place, continue to connect with the place with a sense of commitment and ritual. This can happen in many ways, over weeks, months, or even years. You may already have this kind of habit built into your life as you walk to work, walk your dog, go out to run, visit places for vacations. In this case, it is easy to turn a habit into a sacred ritual by intentionally connecting with this place in reverent and sacred ways as you go about your daily routine of living with or visiting this place.

If visiting your natural place is not easy to do within the flow of your life, try not to pressure yourself to return. Go when you can, or for short periods of time. As discussed in earlier chapters, connecting with nature can be as easy and quick as touching and speaking briefly with the same tree every time you walk by. When we are very busy, connecting with nature can be an easy, supportive, relaxing, peaceful activity.

If your special place is not close enough to visit on a frequent basis, try to visit it in each season, noticing the changes in yourself and the land. In between, you can rely on the friendships that you develop with nature beings that you encounter each day. Because connecting with land helps us become more cyclical, we can support this connection by making our visits cyclical in some way. While creating an intention to visit regularly is helpful, don't let it become stressful. This is a "soft" practice. Feeling nature requires a softening of our bodies and minds; not a forced push into something, but a receptive exchange. This is about just being, so if it's too stressful, wait for another time.

EXERCISE: Connecting with Nature Beings in Your Sacred Place

Purpose

This meditation supports tuning in to aspects of beings in nature that may not be immediately perceivable. We "tune in to" these "invisible" aspects of natural beings by gazing with soft focus, or feeling with soft emotional states. We are watching for life force and learning the energetic imprint of nature beings through coming to feel the teleology of their unfolding on individual and species levels. This meditation is adapted from one offered by Rudolf Steiner, in his book *How to Know Higher Worlds*.[57]

Description

Begin by choosing a nature being to relate to during this meditation (Steiner's meditation suggests using a seed). I have found this method to be effective throughout nature (it even works with people, but for now we will choose something that we think of as nature: stick, leaf, stone, river, tree, cloud, moon). Always ask the being if it is willing to relate with you in this way and wait for a feeling or a sense that it is open to this interaction. Give thanks for the exchange and invite the being to reveal itself to you. Relate to the being with all of your senses.

To begin, if you are a seeing person, watch them with a soft gaze over an extended period of time. Another option is to feel into the being from your heart, intentionally opening to it with love. Once you have established a connection, allow yourself to imagine the natural forces contained in it. Set the intention and imagine that you are sensing the animating life force. Think about the forces that created this being, and what impact it has on the world around it. What internal life forces will form it into something else? How does this being receive the world and how does it press into or bump up against the world? Stare at, or feel into the being until your perceptions begin to shift and you notice something in the being that you have not noticed before; a form, a shape and impression, or a pattern of difference in depth. Sometimes you may see light interacting differently with the being. You may begin to notice connections of energy between this being and other beings around it. Stay engaged with the being until you perceive something new in it that you have not yet perceived. Invite the being to reveal its nature to you. Practice this meditation again and again and you can have surprising and magical relationships, and share stories, between yourself and beings in nature.

EXERCISE: The Ecophenomenology of Rocks

Purpose

Ecophenomenology invites sensual interaction in the moment with the world around us. This ecophenomenology of rocks exercise engages the mind and body to question our assumptions and perceive nature and the world with a fresh perspective. Participants are invited to connect with beings in nature by observing their patterns and rhythms in space and time.

Phenomenology offers a unique perspective that supports ecological consciousness. It provides a conceptual framework that encourages us to abandon our classification of the world as "objects." Releasing the abstractions that we use to filter our experiences allows us to open to a more embodied attentiveness to the world.

Description

When working as a facilitator, or in my own spiritual practice, I usually choose rocks for this practice. They bring millennia of patterns, rhythms and relationships to space and time into any location or room. Working with them offers a depth of opportunity to expand our notions of natural rhythms that few other beings offer.

Begin by holding the rock. When I facilitate this experience, I use a basket of rocks to begin the experience, inviting each participant to tune in to their bodies and intuition, ground to the Earth and choose one. For personal practice, you can create a collection of your own to work with (see "Creating a Set of Sacred Stones," from Chapter Six).

When seeking a phenomenological encounter with a rock (or any being in nature), we begin by clearing our minds of preconceived notions. After "connecting" with the rock for about five minutes, by relating to texture, color, temperature, taste and smell, think of words that you would not usually use to describe a rock. In a group, I ask participants to share these words.

Often, when first seeing a rock we may go to the reductionist concepts and explanations we have come to rely on to categorize phenomena. We tend to think "rock," and move on. If we have geological knowledge, we may classify or name the rock. The Western use of language tends to take the mind automatically to stored conceptual abstractions. Taking an ecophenomenological approach, we begin by releasing these preconceived ideas. Of course, they will all arise. Notice these ideas, then take a breath and look at and feel your rock again.

Relate to the rock. Meditate on the rock. Notice images that you see in the cracks, crevices, and textures of the rock. Consider its time. Where has it come from? Where has it been? Imagine its history and evolution up to this point. Speculate on its age. Do you notice patterns in the rock? How are the patterns of the rock similar or different to the patterns of other beings of nature living nearby? How might these patterns interact? What are the natural rhythms of the rock? How are these rhythms similar or different to other beings living nearby? Are the patterns and rhythms supportive between the rock and its nearby neighbors? Do you notice any possible breakdown in the patterns, movement, time, history or story of the rock?[58]

Close this experience by journaling, drawing or sharing your experiences in a group. Try not to rush to analysis of your experience, but to let it linger in states of sensing. As a facilitator, a good way to open a discussion is to ask the question, "What did you notice?"

My Special Place: The Chagrin River

I jump across the stones over twelve feet of six-inch water. The stones are too far apart and my feet always get wet. Up the dirt horse-track, I step over another trickling creek. I continue up a gravel trail. My lungs pump with my legs and heart as I wind around, past the deer trail, through the cool of the pine grove. Fallen logs fan out through the trees to my right. A little further; down the old moss-covered stone steps into the gulch and across the wooden footbridge, then a scramble down a steep hill. I see a few small swirling pools and smell the fallen leaves, soft and wet under the drizzle. As I turn around a large stone, step over the fallen log, old with decay, the bright, wet green of the ferns against the brown and orange greets me. Another scramble down sliding rocks, most as big as my hand, and I'm there: A wet rock, covered with moss and rain. I sit, damp soaking through my jeans, and watch the water fall in a channel and spread across the wall of slate, separating, coming back together, spraying, washing, gathering leaves, swirling them into patterns.

I like to watch the river. When I say "the river," I mean any river, though all rivers share something that is RIVER. RIVER speaks to me, guides me, teaches me, flows through me. I make friends with individual rivers and have visited one, and its surrounding brooks, regularly for the past decade. As my children have gotten older, and when I have time, I visit the river once a week. Last summer, I visited almost every day for a month and sat for long hours watching and feeling her flow. In northeast Ohio, relating to the planetary spirit of RIVER also means relating with slate and shale, spreading into broad sheets and back again as it winds its way across the face of our watershed.

When I watch the river, I try to do it for a long time. An hour at least, if I can. While I watch the river, I also watch myself. Sometimes I come to see myself much more clearly as I watch the river. Just like the river, my thoughts flow over bumps and grooves, new waters of thought finding common directions over the grooves in the river bed of my mind and body memories. Being with the river helps me be with myself. Other times, when I get very calm, I move more deeply into watching the river. I choose a place in the river and I concentrate on that place for as long as I can sit, looking deeply into the river to see its nature. As time passes, my vision shifts. I come to see that *what I first saw in the river was only a very little of what is there, within, on and surrounding the river. Nothing metaphysical here, just that while at first I saw the spray, watching deeply I come to see that there are layers of spreading water, leaves, contours of rock that I didn't see for a very long time. Light moves in new ways, forming new patterns and reflections all around.*

When I start watching the river, I see what I decide to see. As I sit with the river, the river begins to show me the many layers I have missed with my preconceptions. While watching the spray, I missed the line of tiny leaves on the rocks just below. After a time, vision shifts again so that I see the small trickle slipping under the spray into a private pool. Under the trickle are the wet stones that shape the form of the water, and so on, until the small circle of river appears as a deep, complex interconnected world of its own.

Finding our ground, knowing our ground, is enhanced through creative relationship with the land. The next chapter illustrates the overlap between Earth-connected awareness and creativity. Earth-connected cultures use rituals involving art forms to express, teach and support their connection with nature. The following exercises integrate art as spirituality into rituals that support connecting with nature. Through these rituals, you will begin to integrate creativity as a gateway to ecological consciousness.

8

Nature Art Rituals: Earth-Connecting through Creativity

Creativity is a lovely cousin of Earth-connected consciousness. Both are embedded within the layered matrices of our early learning, and are primary modes of relating, knowing, connecting and expressing. Creativity can "open a side door" to Earth-connected consciousness by supporting a shift from rational ways of knowing. They each have their own related logic and kind of knowing that uses the emotional, symbolic, aesthetic and sensing realms as an avenue for learning. Creative moments are intimately connected with experiences of awe, and often accompany flashes of brilliant vision that offer new ways of seeing the world. Thomas Berry, in *The Dream of the Earth*, describes "spirit power" as expressing more through symbols than words:

> *The new cultural coding that we need must emerge from the source of all such codings, from revelatory vision that comes to us in those special psychic moments, or conditions, that we describe as "dream." We are, of course, using this term not only as regards the psychic processes that take place when we are physically asleep, but also as a way of indicating an intuitive, nonrational process that occurs when we awaken to the numinous powers ever present in the phenomenal world about us, powers that possess us in our high creative moments. Poets and artists continually invoke these spirit powers, which function less through words than through symbolic forms.* [59]

Earth-connected cultures use rituals involving art forms to express, teach and support the awe inherent in feeling the interwoven fabric of the lifeworld. For many of these cultures, the embeddedness with nature that they celebrate is not a "connection," which implies separation of the human from nature, but an experienced fact of self and community, also rarely separated. Paintings, music, dances, costumes representing animals and other forms, many of which have become something that we enjoy as observers, can become part of our daily rituals of healing and celebration of our relationship with nature.

Nature Art Rituals in Sacred Places

You can support your connection with your special place, or with any place, by creating small nature structures. When building in nature, the act itself becomes a ritual of connection with the world around you. Touch, feel, smell, vision and embodied awareness of space become sacred movements celebrating life. Creating structures in nature also connects us with archetypal and instinctual memories of making our lives outside. Often, when building or creating in nature, deep feelings of connection, memory and "home" can emerge. These feelings can feel new and powerful for those who haven't experienced them before. They can also feel extremely normal in the moment, only showing their transformative power when we return to our "normal" world and realize that we are sensing and experiencing differently.

Art works in nature can be big or small. As the creation and building emerges, be sensitive to the natural habitats and other visitors of the area. It is important that the impact is respectful, and even reversible if that is necessary.

EXERCISE: Simple Sacred Nature Art

Purpose

Collecting nature beings for any kind of nature art is soothing and satisfying to the soul. Doing so with the intention of making each movement sacred expands the process into a spiritual practice. Creating with a small collection from nature can be very pleasing to the senses and bring you "down to Earth" for some time among the small world at dirt level that keeps our ecosystems functioning. Collecting rocks, leaves or sticks that seem to you to share a pattern or a symmetry and arranging them in any way that is pleasing to your aesthetic sensibilities enhances your connection with your special place or any place, and with yourself.

Description

Creating nature art in your own sacred nature place, inside or out, expands atrophied natural senses. Touching, smelling, arranging and otherwise relating to patterns and rhythms in nature, we find our own natural rhythms as they are intertwined with life. If you can't get to your special place, you can do this activity any time and anywhere to help you slow down and realign with life. These activities do not require any artistic abilities. Often, simple, quick and easy shapes are the best place to start. Just making circles and circles within circles is healing and enriches our participation with our ecological community.

Creating very simple shapes can bring unexpected balance, healing and clarity. This happens because it taps into parts of our mind/body/spirit that are often neglected. Collect any natural objects/beings that are pleasing to you. Place them into piles, sculptures, circles or spirals. This is one of the kinds of activities, mentioned earlier in the book, that seem too simple to achieve much, but because we are fostering something unrelated to achieving we find our way to completely different kinds of results. As you work, remain conscious of respecting the growth and homes of living things.

If you are creating nature art in a sacred space in your home, go on a foraging expedition for nature beings to bring inside, or create simple nature art with collections that you already have. Making circles and mandalas, or other arrangements, with your set of sacred stones is a quick and easy daily practice to remain grounded to the Earth and maintain contact with the stone beings in your care.

EXERCISE: Working with Ancient Symbols
Purpose

Nature art rituals often begin with ancient symbols that reflect humans' understanding of and relationship with the world and the cosmos. Stacks, circles, spirals and mandalas are highly effective symbols for healing and integration, and have been throughout known human history. They are symbolic "messages from the gods," reminding us that we are in the cosmos and the cosmos is in us. They capture the essence of our place in community with all of life.

Stacks: stacking leaves, or sticks, brings simple joy and develops many aspects of community relationship with the Earth and, if done in a group, with others. Working with pebbles, stones, pine cones, leaves, of either all the same or different colors and shapes sensitizes us to rhythms, consistencies and natural patterns and cycles of growth and decay. You can also build in a creek, with care to not overly disturb the creek bed. Stacking in water, building small dams and waterfalls, watching what you create change in relation to Earth, air or water opens channels to ancient archetypes of the human psyche.

Circles: Circles can add an element of order and aesthetic meaning to nature art projects. Tiny circles, many tiny circles within circles, overlapping circles or larger circles big enough for a person or a group to get inside creates an energy center that can be used as the end in itself, or a "container" for ritual and shamanic work. Circles are an ancient representation of the self and deepen the reflective experience of building in nature. There is no need to try to understand the meaning of building a circle in nature. Immerse yourself in the experience of creating and allow your mind to wander freely. Often, unexpected insights and integrations will occur during or after this process as creativity and nature come together.

Spirals: Spirals are another symbol to work with in nature (think labyrinths). Building spirals adds an element of complexity that can turn collecting and building projects into symbolic experiences. Each spiral is an energetic imprint and has its own relationship with the landscape. Each spiral tells a story, and often strong feelings come up during the process of creating them.
Spirals can be any size, large or small. Spirals can be arranged using leaves, sticks, pine cones, pebbles, rocks or dirt, or can be drawn into soft sand and dirt, or stepped out in the snow. Begin your spiral from the inside and work out, creating the spiral with your hands, feet or sticks used as tools. To deepen

the experience, create a spiral large enough to walk into and out of. Large spirals can be walked on, like labyrinths, in a meditative fashion.

Mandalas: to make an even more complex image, use either similar or different objects and create a mandala. Mandalas have profound symbolic and spiritual significance, and can support our evolving awareness and sensations in relation to nature. To create a mandala, start with a circle of some kind, made from any natural objects/beings that you have collected. To deepen the connection of the mandala with natural cycles, orient the four "corners" of the mandala in what we call the cardinal directions (north, south, east and west). Put something that you have collected directly in the center and create four quadrants, evenly spaced around the circle. We will talk in more detail about creating meditation mandalas in Chapter Fifteen when discussing medicine wheels.

> *While building your mandalas, be prepared for intense feelings, of joy, sadness, excitement, grief. Mandalas can be unexpectedly transparent windows into the emotional and psychological inner world. If sadness or other "uncomfortable" feelings emerge, allow them to be in the circle. There is no need to fix or resolve them.*
>
> *Making mandalas can be a form of self-directed art therapy and may bring up aspects and feelings of the self that have been previously hidden or unknown. You can draw and write your feelings down and let them move through you until they shift. If they feel overwhelming to the point that it feels difficult to function, or if trauma memories emerge, I recommend seeking professional help from a licensed psychotherapist.*

EXERCISE: Spiral Meditation

Purpose

Creating large works of art in nature allows interaction with our bodies within the structure of the art works. One of my ongoing practices is to create large spirals that can be used for personal or group walking meditations. I create spirals with leaves, rocks, sticks and pine cones, or by making tracks in the dirt or snow. Making the spiral is healing when alone and builds community in a spontaneous tribal way when done in a group. When working with others, you can build one spiral together and take turns walking that spiral as a meditation while standing to witness the process for each other, or each build your own spirals near one another.

Creating walking meditation spirals in this way is a simplified form of labyrinth work. Through creating and walking the spirals in nature, we become embodied and embedded in an ancient symbol of the path of spiritual awakening in human form. Moving to the center of the spiral is a way of returning to our spiritual center, to the center of life and the cosmos. It embodies the truth that there is a map to help us through the challenges of our lifetimes on Earth, and the guidance of how to walk this path is often given in symbols.

Description

Locate a place in a natural area where you feel safe and connected. You can use practices from the previous two chapters to locate and build a connection with a special place. Once settled and comfortable, identify something to create a spiral with. You can create spirals with large rocks, small rocks, sticks, leaves, pine cones, in the dirt or in the snow. In snow, I use my boots to stamp down the snow, starting in the center and moving out. Alternatively, you can begin in the center, using your hands to arrange the nature beings, or to move leaves or dirt into the shape of a spiral. I usually aim to make the spiral at least as big across as I am tall, with a pathway wide enough to walk into and out of the spiral.

Once the spiral is built, enter the path from the outside. With your first step into the spiral, acknowledge that you are entering sacred space and set an intention for this walk to be for the healing of your life and the world. Then, beginning on the outside, walk slowly toward the center, taking one step for each breath. In the middle you can take some time to set intentions, ask questions, make prayers of thanks, make blessings or just feel the Earth beneath your feet. When you are ready, go back to the outside just as you came, slowly and in line with your breath. Say a prayer or blessing of gratitude as you exit to honor this experience and the spiral as sacred.

EXERCISE: Nature Collage

Purpose

Sometimes the best way is the simplest way, especially when our hearts and minds feel overwhelmed by complexity. Making a nature collage is a very simple way to slow down and reconnect with ourselves and nature. Creating nature collages is ideal if you do not have access to a natural area large enough for a nature art ritual. You can do this exercise either using items collected from nature or by cutting out pictures of nature. Like any nature art, collages begin with collecting, a ritual of joy and reverence in itself. Seeing a reflection of aspects of ourselves within the image that we are creating, we become more aesthetically sensitive and creatively ordered, put together in a new way.

Making art collages can be joyful and fun, bringing up memories of being a child. Making art is a gift we all have for shifting into our feeling perceptual selves, and our "childlike" senses, which are actually our atrophied natural senses. We are born with them, but many of us forget them over time. These senses are essential for developing ecological consciousness, so returning to the childhood pleasures of simple nature art takes on new relevance as we move through the Earth Spirit Dreaming process.

Description

Your supplies for the collage can be as simple as leaves and grass, small rocks and sticks, and some basic art materials such as paper and glue. Before making your collage, spend some time watching for beings in nature that stand out to you. Allow yourself to intuit the right time, place and materials to use for your project. Watch for natural correspondences or patterns that are attracting you. Try not to second-guess a "feeling" about your nature art ritual, even if your feelings seem foolish to you, or too simple to be meaningful.

Once your collage is complete you can meditate with it, watching with a soft gaze for correlations, relationships, colors and shapes while opening your heart to any messages or feelings that emerge for you.

EXERCISE: Plants and Nature Art

Purpose

An added element that can enhance nature art structures is to plant plants with or in them. There are as many ways to do this as there are situations and groups interested in doing it. You can create any kind of nature art in a variety of sizes. Over time, especially if the materials have been put together loosely, or are easily scattered by rain and wind, you can observe how the plants grow as the built structure moves, changes and even rots. Maybe little animals or bugs start munching on or living in the structure, while the plants continue to grow and thrive. This juxtaposition of life and decay, growth, rootedness, movement and change represents a coming together and interrelation of nature cycles.

Description

Any nature art work can be joined together with plants that are already growing, or that you want to plant as a part of your project. You can create temporary or more permanent nature art with plants in pots or in and around a garden.

Another approach is to create a nature art ritual structure that is more permanent, such as a spiral or a mandala garden for vegetables, herbs or flowers. I will give a personal example.

This spring, I am in the process of building a healing mandala garden. The mandala is built in relation to the four directions, with medium stones anchoring the mandala at north, south, east and west. Smaller stones anchor the intermediary directions: northwest, northeast, southwest, southeast. The middle of the mandala is another, smaller circle of stones. The intention for the mandala is to support a personal healing journey of my own, as well as to offer healing for others who visit or add rocks to the garden, and to support healing for the world. Another purpose for the garden is for my children to have a nature art ritual and a garden that they can be a part of creating and caring for. The outer ring of the garden is planted with greens, some small vegetables and herbs, while the center circle of the garden is planted with bulbs that will bloom at different seasons.

I invite my children, neighbors and visitors to add a rock to the center circle, making a wish, setting an intention, or making a prayer. Recently, my children and I began painting little rocks in many different colors and adding them to the garden. What a fun and creative way to continue to relate and grow with the garden! The rock rings change in feel and form as the seeds sprout. The art and the energy transform as the plants grow. It is a living entity.

We balance on the small paths to place the rocks, finding a new sense of our own balance with life. This relationship to balance is an unintentional learning and healing of the mandala, as we are all on tippy-toes trying not to step on the tiny, new plants. When anyone steps toward the center of the garden, they appear to be dancing as they maneuver along the little walking paths. Not surprisingly, this balancing dance with the garden comes more fluidly and easily for the children than it does for me. I watch children move in the garden to learn their ways of walking to the center of the mandala and out again. It is their own labyrinth of learning and growth and it is for me as well.

From earth-connecting, we move next into the spirit-connecting portion of the Earth Spirit Dreaming method. Once we develop the means to increase our ecological consciousness by slowing down and connecting with nature, we create the ground, literally and figuratively, to begin working with vibrational reality. Our newly developed Earth senses support the focus needed to increase our vibrational and spiritual awareness and begin to use them for personal and planetary healing. The next chapter will help readers understand why and how we segue from earth-connecting to spirit-connecting practices at this stage of Earth Spirit Dreaming. As a natural growth from one to another, vibrational awareness evolves from and constitutes part of our perceptual natural senses.

Part 3

Spirit-Connecting Practices

9

Spirit-Connecting: Working with Light and Vibrational Reality

When the idea for this book was born, I meant it to be about Earth-connecting practices only. I did not yet realize the shifts in consciousness that awaited me as a result of these practices. As my commitment to nature-based spiritual practices continued, alongside my writing, what the Earth was teaching me expanded far beyond my expectations. I discovered, and it was revealed to me, that reconnecting with Earth leads to engaging with spiritual reality in ways that I had yet to know through an entire lifetime of spirituality and religion. Over time, and through many adventures, engaging with Spirit on an Earth-based path uncovers a view of human nature that is completely distinct from Western conceptions of the self.

As I follow the life-world beyond the realm of the rational and continue to open and develop my sensitivities to the natural world, the reality that I discover "beyond the realms of reason" blows my mind wide open again and again. Through blocks and fears, joy and wonder, I now often relate to life with a raw, non-linear wildness that is increasingly integrated with my "everyday" experience. Each day I discover that what I think of as "nature" is much more vast, surprising and magical than seems possible in the current Western concept of "the real."

This journey into the realms of the wild mind and body of the Earth began for me with simple nature meditation. I followed my intuition to many of the practices that I share in this book to find my way back to my own ecological consciousness. This Earth-connected consciousness unveiled an enhanced kinesthetic experience of what we might call "energy" throughout nature and people: Connections of light as an expression of the stories and overlapping dreams of all beings between and around us including trees, rocks, animals, moss, rivers and people.

I understand the shift in my perceptions to be a direct result of my many hours of spiritual practice in nature; I understand this expansion of consciousness to be an outcome of directly asking the Earth to teach me how to best live in alignment with life and healing for the world.

In shamanic traditions, it might be said that I began to undergo an initiation, not intentionally sought by me or because of any outside human influences. Rather, this was somehow a result of my commitment to listening to the Earth. I hesitate to use the word "shamanic" because I did not train with a shamanic teacher, an indigenous healer or medicine person, or anyone who might have shown me the path to developing increased levels of shamanic sensation. Despite not intentionally seeking a shamanic path, or even knowing that I was in some way self-guiding myself toward a shamanic awakening, it happened to me. My conclusion from this is that all people can find their way to profound, consciousness-shifting spiritual development through intensive contact with nature and the Earth community. Not everyone's path leads to what I came to see as my spiritual mission: to live as a healer and teacher of these ways. Yet, we can all come to know Earth and Spirit sensitivities, perceptions and practices that can enhance and heal our lives.

Through relearning how to know nature — what Joanna Macy calls "Coming Back to Life" — we can eventually learn to interact directly with nature spirits, ancestors and spirit helpers.[60] To get to that level of communication with these beings in parallel and interrelated realities, we must first learn to experience the web of light that forms among and between all of the stories and dreams of the Earth community. Our minds will never be able to understand or know all that there is in this vast and endless web, as it stretches beyond limits of perception to the outer reaches of the universe. We can, however, begin to perceive and work with this web as it is expressed in an immediate matrix around our own lives and communities.

Over time, as we learn to feel and move in these webs of light we can directly relate to and influence things within this realm. We all have it in us to find these ancient ways of wisdom simply by connecting with the forces of life around us. With time, intention and commitment, we can all "wake up" from our daze of industrial culture.

Portals to Guides in Vibrational Reality

From sitting in circles of rocks over months and years, with intention, song, creativity, movement and prayer, I now know these circles as portals of shifted space that allow communication with other-than-human beings. The first time that I felt this kind of portal, I knew in a softly bubbling flash that rocks hold the original dream of the Earth; they hold space for us to find our way back to the intention of life: to love, relate, create, fall away, become. As this awakening continues to unfold for me, my profound love of nature all around me shifts the air and the air shifts me. Sacred circles, as I now experience them, are a field, a portal and gateway, a channel, a river, of shifted vibrations that alter my perceptions of time and space, and everything about reality that goes with those structures. These shifts in frequency — a limited word that doesn't capture the reality of portals very well — develop over months and years of fostering sacred relationship with specific places. As these vibrational portals grow and develop in relationship with us, they open channels to speak with beings of light that support us in our lives and work as humans. They become contact points, expanded and catalyzed by being a place to invite contact with spirit helpers, nature spirits, benevolent ancestors and the body memories of the Earth.

I know this to be true as others feel the difference when they enter the field of these circles, the shimmering at the edges of perception and the waves of difference in what we feel and know in these sacred Earth-based spirit-doused spaces. Entering a cultivated sacred circle feels like entering a "room," or crossing a threshold into another perceptual field. In this way, I learned what people mean when they say "medicine" wheel; the medicine is the magic that happens when we love life in a sacred way with ancient symbols of wholeness and connection. I found this through decades of working with mandalas, another form of sacred circle and representation of our relationship with the cosmos. Medicine wheels, prayer circles, labyrinths, henges and other forms of sacred circles are cosmic symbols seemingly so simple, they are medicine for humans on a genetic and soul level; these are magic gateways to feeling, knowing and dreaming new dreams; these are maps bearing messages from the Divine on how to navigate the challenges of life on Earth.

Recently, in my teaching as a shamanic ecotherapy practitioner, a planetary guide, named Joseph, has been joining me often to teach, to speak through me and to guide my class.[61] Though I have interacted with spirit helpers and planetary guides in shamanic journeys, this is the first time that I am hearing and feeling one so palpably in a room with me while in a "normal," not trance or just a very light trance, state. And all of my students, some able to sense "energy" and some not, immediately feel him, too. People who have never had shamanic experiences feel Joseph enter the circle. When he enters the room, the quality of his vibration as a being is on such a strongly different frequency that we all feel it. I move around the room working with my students' energy bodies to help them balance their own personal vibrational imprint with Joseph's so that they can remain relatively comfortable and join in in the best way for them. Connecting with Joseph is always a personal choice, and I ask everyone's permission for him to join us. Joseph joins us with respect, a sense of humor, a palpable personality, a commitment to be a part of our circle as a participant. He also comes with a pressure to share his message, which he describes as the transmission of his soul group for the planet and our species.

Joseph says things that none of us can possibly know or imagine from the limits of our human experience. I didn't expect this to happen when I taught Earth Spirit Dreaming for the first time in an immersive context. I always set an intention that my spirit helpers come to help me teach and hold space in alignment for the healing of the world. I sing and play a personal spirit song on a clay flute inviting light beings to come down with wisdom. Apparently, Joseph heard me and took up the invitation. Once again, the results of my intentions to connect with the Earth and spirit realms took me to places far beyond reason and my own expectations. Joseph showing up was never in my mind as a possibility. When it happened I did not want to go there for about two minutes. Then I told my students about Joseph's presence, outed myself as feeling "so weird"[62] to be sharing this completely unexpected experience in this moment and went on with the class.

With a sense of humor, Joseph enters as a "co-teacher" with respect and admiration for the work that we have done to allow him to directly communicate with us. Joseph is funny, intense, powerful, sexy and friendly. Now, Joseph sits with me to help me find the words, often his words, so that I might help my students understand the essential nature of working with light. How this work is so quick, simple and soft compared to functioning or creating in physical reality; how this work is instant, outside of time and space; how the healing light work that we do now can extend behind and before us in time and throughout history to alter things in the present for the world. When I move from visioning through vibrational work to shamanic reality, Joseph moves gently aside to allow other guides to work with me and through me. Supporting humans in shamanic journeying is not his area or his spiritual mission. He respects the other guides and steps aside.

As Joseph works with us, we all move gradually into increasingly intense trance states. My students say that they feel different, and I tell them that we are moving into altered states of perception. It is gradual, and they know that they feel different but they aren't sure how or why. For people who have never experienced this kind of thing, most feel surprisingly comfortable and safe. Joseph is an excellent teacher, able to work with the group and meet all of us where we are. What I don't tell my students is that while Joseph is there, we sometimes experience time slips. He gives me things to do in the last half an hour of class to finish our work and bring everyone back into "this world." I know that we don't have time to do these things. After 30 minutes of work, I look at my timekeeper and see that four minutes have passed in our world. We had entered Joseph's world, where time is fluid.

So, what began as a meditation practice of watching nature and listening to the Earth is now a daily awakening to a level of wildness and magic that surprises me and pushes me beyond my expectations, and out of my mind, more and more each day. This is possible because, together with many others, I am creating a new culture and a new story; we are re-indigenizing. It is through love of place, through caring for our ancestors, through speaking with the Earth, through storytelling within initiated communities of awake adults, that these things happen. This is the result of work with vibrational reality; our bodies shift through working with light so that we can hear voices that we never imagined existed.

Incorporating Revelation into the "Everyday"

The information and experience of heightened spiritual awareness can feel far away, and maybe not even true, in my "everyday" life. Doubt and questioning is normal when opening to magic. This gets better over time, and the veils are thinner with every month and year that I practice. These realities are blended, though blocks from certain kinds of current consensual dreams create thick and heavy resistance to shifting my thought forms and belief structures. The old thought forms are seductive. My body is naturalized to them and quickly returns to ruts of thinking and sensation. It is the work of a lifetime, and requires near-constant vigilance, to dream a healing dream. I often fall out of synch with this commitment and guide myself back again and again. I set reminders and consistent daily practices to bring me back.

Keeping the commitment to sacred Earth spiritual practice is challenging. We don't have the institutions or community structures to support these habits and rituals. Building my own community helps me hold these intentions and continue this work. Through founding an institute to cultivate ecological consciousness and community, I am now often surrounded by people who are committed to a similar journey. *Together*, we create the time, space and rituals to support one another in shifting our collective consciousness. *Together* is the operative word for shifting our consciousness and dreaming new dreams for the Earth. Everything is connected and so must we be to heal and create new stories. The new story for the planet is about community, can only happen in community and rebuilds our communities.

As I now work regularly with light in my meditations and spiritual practices, I am increasingly sensitive to vibrations in every encounter and situation. I notice that I often shift rapidly from a loving space through anger, annoyance, frustration, worry or fear. When I do this, as Joseph teaches, the thought forms and beliefs that exist in our collective consciousness around negative, dark, dense emotions rush in all around me, expanding these heavy states. I lose faith in these moments, and I feel lost. I lose the ability to feel the music of the Divine in my heart-mind.

I find that the habits of mind and body that keep my vibrations dense were, and are, deeply entrenched. If I am not aware at every moment, I will fall into these habitual patterns. Staying in a vibration of light, peace and joy is the hardest thing I have ever done, requires constant mindfulness and is the primary work of my lifetime.

My current practice is to attempt to channel healing light into the world in all that I do. To do this, mindfulness and meditation become essential. I must watch, feel and know my thoughts as often as I can as each one is creative and weaves into the fabric of the stories that are our collective dream. This is easier with time, though "life" often seems to get in the way. Sometimes, the best that I can do is to wake up every morning sending light to everything in my life, and to all of the world, to remind me of what I am doing here. Questions, concerns, fears, quandaries, hopes, dreams, entanglements, illness all get the treatment with love and light that I will teach you here. I used to find the greeting "with love and light" so trite, and now I truly and deeply understand what this means, through the guidance of spirit helpers. Working with light to shift our reality and change the world does not mean that we push our difficult feelings away or shut ourselves down to them. The ability to open our hearts to all feelings is essential to the path of awakening. Working with light, we learn to hold our grief, our pain, our fear, our love, our joy, our hope, and all other emotions, in our own arms with love.

Raising Vibrations: A Full-Time Job

Keeping our vibrations attuned to love feels like a full-time job, yet it is essential in order to come to understand our creative capacity. We are creating our lives and the world in every moment. What I now understand, through my own practice and experience, is that any time we don't maintain a loving, peaceful vibration — when we get caught up in the fears, anger and frustrations of our world — we are supporting thought forms that are damaging. I know deeply the pain and woundedness of the world through my own traumatic early life, through sensitivity to others' pain through a sometimes crippling level of empathy that I've learned to manage and channel as a healer and teacher and through social justice and environmental activism and scholarship. I'm not saying not to see or feel these feelings, but to live deeply into them with love in order to transmute them. By embracing all of ourselves with love, we can call our spirits back from many things that pull us outside of ourselves. In this way, we can learn to embrace our full power as often as we can. When we send our "spirit," our energy, into a situation, it pulls our spirit body away from our center and limits our creative capacities. So, we can acknowledge pain and have compassion, then pull back our spirit and embrace our power to transform these situations through working with light in vibrational reality.

For me personally, Joseph offers the vision of a river. My work with the spirits of rivers comes from many lifetimes ago when my entire meaning in my community was to relate to the river for my tribe. Joseph shows me to be the river when I encounter addictive thought forms. As the river, I touch these thought forms lightly and keep moving, glide past, let myself press the banks when I need to, to get through the tight places and white waters. The Earth will hold me as I create my path to Lake Erie, near my home, and eventually to the sea, the sky, into the web of Gaia, the consciousness of the biosphere.

Still, I get annoyed at my husband, crabby at my kids, sick and depressed, but now I know that I have to not suppress these experiences but hold them in light. I know from 25 years of therapy that suppressing my feelings will do no good. The work is to love completely my sadness, anger, illness, shortcomings and the people who hurt me, abandon me and let me down. This love and work with light allows me to call back my spirit and let the Earth and the light beings all around us transmute that energy through the fire of light back into my source of power emanating from my heart. From the Buddhist perspective we might understand this as a softness and compassion toward all things rough in the world, but also there is a vibrational level of reality through which we can actually transmute these energies into something else. My lifetime trauma with my mother is now transmuted into a new energy and power to heal through the great feminine energies of the planet, and to begin to understand and incorporate the healthy masculine energies as well. To be on the planet in a new way is a new choice every day. I am often tempted into old patterns and stories. The work of the rest of my life is to inhabit this vibrational wisdom, a great gift from enlightened beings, for which I am grateful beyond all else.

Karmic Eddies

One day, as often happens while I am meditating, a new awareness came to me. I received an image that has helped me to better support my goal of raising my vibrations and bringing light to the world for healing. I did not come up with this idea: it is a gift. This gift helps me unwind many of the discordant, unbalanced, trauma-induced matrices of my body, heart and mind. The idea is an image of karmic eddies.

As I often do in gifts from the spirit wisdom moments, I received this image while gazing at a river. I am intimately connected with the intelligence of River. For this reason, I was especially open to and inspired by this new way of seeing River as a guide. In the karmic eddy image, I see my life as a river of light flowing through a quiet wood. Along the sides of the river are eddies where my energy flows, swirls and sometimes stops, circling around and around on issues that are mine to work through and resolve in this life. Some I brought with me, and some are pains and puzzles I carry to grow my soul on this particular journey to

Earth. Though the work of a certain eddy might be done, I still find myself spinning around and around in these offshoots of the river of myself. Karmic eddies can pull me from my work of fulfilling my spiritual mission with my full and present self. The gift of this image is to help me find ways to work through and release these issues in my life. In the next chapter, I will describe specific practices that I have discovered through meditation to relieve some of the hold of these spinning pools. I don't force myself out of them, but seek awareness of them; they are often unconscious. As I work over time with my karmic eddies, I become increasingly aware of the ways in which they pull me away from my task of remaining mindful of my vibrational state.

Creating Mindfully in Vibrational Reality

The longer I explore the vibrational web of life, the more I see the overlapping weave of the vibrations that our personal and collective stories create. Sometimes, I can remain aware for most of a day of my role in these vibrational interactions. When I am stressed and unconsciously living from old patterns, I pray that my guides will nudge me to remind me to pivot toward conscious dreaming when most needed.

Another gift of wisdom that I know from continuing to work on my vibrational presence in the world is that we are either sending or receiving in vibrational reality. Early in my life, I had taken a class on psychic boundaries to help me manage my intense level of sensitivity to the "stuff" of other people, energetic fields and entities. I know methods to "protect" myself from incoming vibrations of energies that seek to attach to and pull from my life force. The new image and understanding of karmic eddies teaches me something more useful and important. This new understanding surpasses the idea of protection with a responsibility to acknowledge my co-creation of story-making in and with the web of life in every moment. I now know that I am part of actively dreaming into being the fabric of the world. While it is okay, and even good, to protect ourselves, I have discovered that in every moment I can influence the vibrations around me. My spirit helpers have taught me that when

I am neutral or protecting myself, I am essentially giving up my power as a conscious dreamer and co-creator of the story of the Earth. Instead of deflecting vibrations with my hard-earned boundaries, I can actively transform them by holding them in light with my open and authentic heart-mind. I can change the world in every moment, which is breathtaking, awe-inspiring and also intimidating. To be healers of the world, we cannot hide; we are dreaming the dream of the Earth — the story of humans on and with the Earth — right now, yesterday, tomorrow, into the past and the future, always.

Committing to a Path of Awakened Dreaming

Working with vibrations requires consciously birthing our stories in every moment, as the network of energy within and behind our "normal" reality is a collection of interwoven stories of all beings everywhere. If you feel called to heal the world, and take part in bringing our species back into balance with the Earth, I strongly encourage you to ground to the Earth, speak to the Earth and open to the teachings and life-altering shifts that come through this potent practice. The sudden shifts in awareness and feelings that arise when changing our stories to shift our vibrations can be intense. Grounding and learning to watch our own mind by developing connection with our spirit selves as witnesses and guides of our Earth body selves helps support this process of change that shifts every aspect of our being. Simultaneously, our Earth body selves guide our spirit and call forth our reason for being on the planet at this time.

Often in Western culture we want to rush to new experiences, new spiritual realities, new levels of consciousness, without building the ground to make these activities safe and effective over time. To shift our inner and outer worlds is a profound commitment that requires personal transformation on the deepest levels. Because Western culture does not support development of these abilities throughout life, we must understand that we are children in this realm compared with many indigenous cultures that maintain these kinds of knowledge through their daily personal and community habits and rituals. Committing to building skill, strength, grounding and awareness is essential to doing the work that is healing for ourselves and the world.

After 20 years of Earth-connected spiritual practice, I am now just a beginner in my work in non-ordinary realities. I am deeply humbled by my experiences in vibrational and spiritual realities (these are not separate) and move with great respect and gratitude through this work, asking for direction, protection and support, and giving great thanks for these, on a regular basis. I know more than ever that this is a profound work, a Great Work, as Thomas Berry says, the work of lifetimes to change the course of humanity through desperate challenges.[63]

Vibrational awareness and energy-shifting techniques are effective in changing your life and the world immediately. It can be astounding to experience the changes that can occur by merely shifting the direction and quality of our stories, beliefs and energetic engagement with the world. Take it slowly as you move through the vibrational awareness exercises in the coming chapters of this book. Remember to connect often with your body and the Earth to ground the expansions and sometimes rapid changes that inevitably come.

In the upcoming chapters, I share methods for raising vibrations, bringing healing light to all situations, big or small, working with karmic eddies and transforming situations through continual conscious creation of our stories. The next series of practices guides readers through the preparatory stages for working in energetic and vibrational, and eventually shamanic, experience. The next chapter gives clear guidelines for utilizing the Earth-connecting practices, from the previous section, to support the expansion into vibrational and spiritual work safely and effectively.

10

Sacred Space and Preparation for Working with Light

One person living consciously in vibrations of light can truly change the world. One person living fully into new and healing stories, from love and alignment with life, can wash over and transmute many negative, destructive feelings, beliefs and thought forms. Once we are in light, we connect with others who are dreaming the world from similar vibrations, and we create a consciousness, a channel, of visionary dreaming that makes it easier for all of us to maintain healing dreams. I cannot state often enough the daily work, mindfulness and consistent practice that goes into holding these visions for a new world; sickness, exhaustion, grief, unexpected personal and world events can throw us off, and throw me off much of the time. Still, we get back up and start with just one more thought of light. When in doubt, I start shifting to a higher vibration by counting my blessings. If they are hard to come by in a given moment, I start by thanking God for my breath, then for the air, then for the trees, then for the sun and Earth that nourish the trees, just one more grateful thought at a time. Even for pain, for darkness, for shadow, we find gratitude. All of life is sacred in all of her forms. We come to honor this through great feats of mind-shifting over and over again.

The following practices support the joining of our Earth and Spirit selves. Awakening to our full potential as connected beings with our Earth and Spirit communities, with clear intention, we can vision lives and a world of beauty, care, creativity, justice and love. Waking up to our full selves, we come into our ancestral knowledge that we are dreaming the world into being in every moment, with every thought and every emotional imprint that we bring forth into form. This section of the book invites mindfulness, as we work to hold a vision of connection with the Earth. We choose consciously to focus on gratitude, love and healing in order to vision the world into light. The dominant energies on our planet are often not conducive to these visions of healing. We must watch carefully our tuning in to the news, gossip, family drama, negative thought patterns, that are reaching out to us constantly from every direction. The more we see light and beauty, the more we draw it toward us and bring it forth in the world.

How to Know Vibrational Reality

Practicing the Earth-connecting activities in Part Two of this book will support working with vibrational reality. The longer and more consistently we work with the Earth-connecting practices, the more facility we develop for working with vibrational energy. When we move into working with energetic/vibrational reality, we can create a picture of ourselves rooted to the Earth and connecting with Spirit. Visualizing this truth helps us develop an embodied knowing that we are beings of Earth and Spirit, and thus can blend and move through these realms with sensitivity and intention. Deepening these practices, we move from unconscious to conscious creation.

Our rational mind rejects the sensations of the practices; we have a little Descartes in our heads telling us that our mental concepts of reality represent truth, and to distrust the other-than-rational knowing of our bodies and spiritual perceptions that often fail to fit neatly within that rational framework. Ironically, embodied, spiritual experience shows us that our thoughts are creating truth; in that sense, Descartes was right — "I think, therefore I am" is truer than he knew, albeit with a completely different slant. Rather than our thoughts accurately reflecting objective reality "out there," it is the truth of our inner experience, expressed in thoughts, that empowers us to co-create the world "out there" through intentional, heart-informed thinking. Joseph again: "Your current problems arise because your minds have come to instruct your hearts. The shift now is for your hearts to give directions to your minds."[64] This is moving back into our bodies and hearts, and activating an adjusted alignment with the skills of our rational minds.

Words are very limited for describing experiences with energy and light and can distort our ideas of these other realms. Instead, we are required to move beyond the limits of our language to learn the special ways of knowing available to us in vibrational, spiritual reality. Yet, words are what we have to share these experiences until we can share by connecting to one another in those realms, which does begin to happen with shamanic healers and long-time spiritual practitioners. After long practice, our understanding is seated more and more in our heart-mind, which speaks in symbols, feelings, intuitions and story. Only this symbolic part of ourselves, our wisdom self (archetypal self), can "understand" energetic and spiritual forces. While the Western paradigm champions rational thinking, and rational thinking has grown human knowledge in tremendous and valuable ways, it is time to reawaken our symbolic, Earth-connected heart wisdom.

Preparing to Work with Light in Vibrational Reality

Our vibrational awareness is connected to, and inseparable from, our emotional, mental and physical bodies. While attempting to separate ourselves into various aspects and systems — mind, body, spirit, psyche, soul — is a limitation of Western language, these concepts provide useful maps. These maps, however, are merely guides that are unable to capture our wholeness as integrated beings. Developing ecological consciousness, we understand that as nothing in the world is ultimately separate from anything else, so none of our "parts" are separate from one another. As we move fully into Earth Spirit Dreaming, we embody the truth that everything is connected. Cultivating reverence for life — through ceremony, creativity, learning a sacred and intuitive flow with Earth   we create sacred space to open gateways to vibrational experience.

Our subtle energy system, the origin of our ability to perceive vibrational fields, is deeply integrated with all of the other systems of our bodies as well as the life systems of the planet. Awareness of vibrations is interlinked with our sensitivity to physical and emotional sensation. Thus, our physical and emotional sensations can guide us toward a deeper understanding of vibrational reality. Eventually, this changes the way that we experience and understand our thinking. For that reason, it is helpful, and strongly encouraged, to always start with an embodying Earth-connected practice from the previous section of the book before actively engaging with vibrational fields. It is important to do vibrational work with as much clarity and conscious intention as possible, and as much connection with Earth through our bodies as we can foster in any given sacred dreaming experience. It is essential to be strongly grounded, and to clear your physical and emotional space before working with vibrational fields. Without this preparation, we are inevitably pulled into an ingrained tendency to entrain with the dominant fields surrounding us, rather than transforming and lightening consciousness in ourselves and the world.

Preparation and clear intention lead to active awakening to our creative and healing abilities as spiritual beings. Take time to prepare; again, take time to prepare. The basis of the Earth Spirit Dreaming method is that we become aligned with our evolutionary, genetic full selves: That all of our gifts and ways of knowing are attuned to the profound task at hand. We enter the work of dreaming initiated into fullness as humans and as much completeness of alignment with Earth and Spirit as we can muster in any given moment. Though we are never as far as we might go next time, we practice, practice, practice with dedicated intent to bring forth a new world. Preparation is the most important part of the work: creating the gate, learning to let it open, stepping through to consciously dream and envision the world anew.

Michael Laitman captures beautifully the mystery and humbling wonder of working in vibrational light fields in his book, *A Glimpse of Light: The Basics of the Wisdom of Kabbalah:*[65]

> *I am in a large, expansive system, which I don't feel or understand.*
> *In that tremendous system, I live in a tiny place called "this world."*
> *How do we reveal the entire system, know it all, feel it all, and*
> *become its owner?*

Drawing the Light within the system is the force that will open up my senses, my inner channels, the force of life that will restore my consciousness.[66]

We begin our preparation to enter the light realms with awareness and intention by creating sacred space, the groundwork of opening gateways to cross the threshold of reason into conscious perception of light.

EXERCISE: Creating Sacred Space

Purpose

To support your practice working with healing vibrations and light, first create a sacred space and set a clear intention. There are many ways to create sacred space and it is important to find a method that feels right to you. Trust your intuition, and all of your fully developed natural senses, to lead you to the methods that will be personally powerful and connective. You can do this by exploring rituals for creating sacred space, then improvising from these methods until you find the elements of ritual that work. To do this, by following the guidance in this exercise, find your own sacred objects, rituals and places that tell your body and mind that you are now entering a deep spiritual place, opening to vibrational awareness, a practice to re-vision your life and the world.

Through regular practice, your own sacred space and personal ceremonial cues will help you reach gateways to spiritual-vibrational reality more quickly and dependably. Also, whatever space and place you choose to do this work will become increasingly "charged" for you, and those who you may choose to invite into the sacred work. Your rituals, sacred place and ceremonial objects will become a reservoir of strength and insight for you.

Description

Begin to create sacred space with the locations and tools that you worked with for the Earth-connecting practices earlier in this book. The connections and cues to your body to wake up and engage with ecological consciousness is the first element of effectual vibrational work for healing the world.

> Eventually, your sacred space becomes the landscape for shamanic visioning. Creating sacred space comes from an intention to do things in a sacred way.
>
> Compose an altar with sacred objects: things that bring you positive feelings of joy, gratitude and love; special and meaningful memories; and beloved places.
>
> Also, collect things from nature. Locate your altar in a place that feels safe and special to you. Choose a beautiful cloth for it. Arrange the altar with great care, feeling the relationship between all of the sacred things, holding each one in gratitude and allowing a web to form between them.
>
> You can create circles of objects and stones honoring the directions, and add things to honor earth, wind, fire and water; the species of the world such as feathers from the winged ones, water beings with shells, earth walkers, herbs, sacred plants and trees, or any other aspects of the world community. And, it is okay and just right to start where you are, even with just a few sacred things and a small shelf or place on the floor. Altars grow and shift over time. The most important thing is to begin and cherish the process with as many things and any space that you can find.
>
> Keep the objects and this place in a sacred way and interact with them from a place of beauty. Send this space light, love and gratitude as often as you can. Loving objects changes the charge and meaning of these things in our lives and sacred work. If possible, use these objects and this place only for spiritual work.

Eventually your sacred space and objects will signal to your body, mind and spirit that it is time to enter your spiritual work. Over time, your body will learn to catalyze with the signifiers more quickly and deeply. These repeat patterns help you get to the appropriate state of consciousness quickly and effectively. Repetition of routines that create a grounded and clear space support the practice of vibrational work.

This is where rituals come in. The components and order of activities that create a preparation ritual for vibrational/energy work will be different for everyone, but often start with sacred locations and sacred objects. You can work with various exercises and ideas from the previous chapters and those later in the book, as well as weaving in other activities that activate your sense of awe.

Experiment with a process that feels good to you, then improvise within this framework to keep it fresh and in line with your growth. Clear your thoughts through quiet time, meditation, journaling — again, whatever works to clear the clutter. If you need guidance, try the suggestions for ceremonies in Chapter Two of this book.

EXERCISE: Grounding to the Earth

Purpose

The importance of grounding, and why we do it as part of an integrated spiritual practice, is the Earth-connecting aspect of this method. It is important to ground every time we open sacred space to vibrational healing work for ourselves or for others. Eventually the goal is to feel grounded to the Earth throughout our lives, and definitely any time we are doing spiritual practices. Grounding to the earth becomes a daily part of living in an ecologically conscious way. To ground you can use any of the exercises from the Earth-connecting section of this book.

Along with developing an awareness of grounding throughout your life and spiritual development, choose a place within any ceremony to intentionally ground and honor the Earth and all of life. I usually do this a few times in different ways in each ceremony. Where you do it is not particularly important, but doing it is essential to work with vibrational and shamanic reality safely and effectively.

Description

Often before I create or enter sacred space I feel my foot on the ground, and go barefoot on the Earth if I am outside; or I imagine a cord reaching from the base of my spine where I am sitting down into the core of the Earth through any simple visualization that comes to me in the moment. Also, I work with stones as sacred objects, as mentioned throughout this book, to help me ground, and often place stones on my body or rest my feet on stones during rituals and healing work.

I consciously ground as soon as I begin any ceremony or ritual, and often before. If I am preparing a ceremony in a new place, I will ask the Earth to show me where and how to connect with the energetic patterns and elementals in a particular location. Hold grounding as an intention as often as you can. This will come naturally as a result of regular Earth-connecting practices. Always find a place in your ceremonies to intentionally ground your sacred space to the Earth. The more time we give to preparing — grounding, clearing, setting our intention — the more impactfully will our vibrational and visioning experiences translate into the world over time.

EXERCISE: Setting Clear Intentions
Purpose

Like the physical world, the world of vibrations is filled with a wide variety of information, experience and drama. Becoming actively engaged and intentional with our action in this realm is essential to bring healing and transformation to our lives and our world. Before entering an energetic/vibrational experience (after embodied grounding), be clear about your intention for the practice.

In the vibrational realm, many of us are programmed by our experience in Western culture to take, to pull energy through wanting and longing. One of our guiding cultural norms is to consume, and we are often thinking about what we can get, and what we need, even if we don't realize we are thinking about it. Pulling energy is often unconscious: I need more money, who will care for me if I'm sick, where will I live. This underlying and insidious insecurity perpetuated by the dominant global consciousness can influence our work with vibrations. Whether we know it or not, we are always moving through the world of vibrations. Seemingly paradoxically, we are able to lighten and clear our energy at a vibrational level by giving, rather than pulling.

The energy of giving — love, light, positive intention — increases (raises) our vibration and allows us to connect with other souls with high vibrations, and open a channel to higher beings that want to support our spiritual growth. With this in mind, when setting intentions for working with energy, your work will be more effective if you set your intention with a goal of giving.

Carefully reflect on and consider your intentions for spiritual work. We can unintentionally perpetuate our old stories and patterns through our intentions. When we ask for specific things, it's important to know that we may not be surrendering to our spirit for our own best growth and healing. Often, what is best for our spiritual development and growth feels uncomfortable and scary. Yet, we also need to keep our day-to-day lives in balance. So, it is a careful balancing act to set intentions for healing ourselves and the world and honoring our own agency to open to this in a way that we can handle. Our spirit guides are eager to help us grow, which can feel overwhelming and beyond our ability to manage sometimes. It takes time to grow our capacity for letting go of many of the things that feel safe and most relevant in our lives.

It is okay to say no and set limits, and also good to create intentions that support healing. Sometimes, if this feels too hard, we can stay neutral in our spiritual work, simply asking for support and wisdom to get through a day or a period of our lives. When I set an intention, I do my best to let go of the outcomes, while also identifying my bottom line and setting that within the parameters of my intention. For example, my intention is to fulfill my spiritual mission on the planet to the best of my ability. My bottom line for my Earth self is that I want to give my children a stable home and live in a warm, safe house with my furniture and my friends nearby.

Description

Create a daily prayer that is a general intention for your life, and then create individual intentions within that when you do specific pieces of work. Taking the time to create a general intention that is informing your life becomes a good guide to lean on when life is very busy or becomes unexpectedly difficult.

My daily prayer of intention for many years was, "Divine Creator of the Universe, what can I most be to glorify you?" My always prayer now is, "I pray that my life will be in alignment with my soul mission and the healing of the world." This can be a scary prayer, as things that my ego is very attached to have fallen away or been transformed beyond recognition. But, these shifts in my life have opened me up to levels of healing, peace and joy that I wouldn't have imagined possible. So, instead of asking for this or that thing to work out (which of course we all do sometimes, anyway), it helps to reframe concern for individual issues into a giving, flexible approach when possible. That said, when things get really hard I still sometimes fall on my knees and beg-pray for help and for certain outcomes.

11

Opening to Vibrational Reality

Our personal vibrations emanate from our conscious and unconscious beliefs about ourselves, others and the world. Very often, we are sending and receiving energy to areas of our lives and the world without awareness. Nonetheless, these choices, even when unconscious, constitute our participation in creating our lives and the world as we know them. We also often give away our spiritual power, the life force of our energy bodies, by extending our energy and life force to thoughts, feelings and situations that drain us. By learning to work consciously with our vibrations, we can restore our own health and spiritual power, and actively participate in healing the world.

Just as we need to develop fluid boundaries for our physical and emotional selves, it is equally important to learn to manage the boundaries of our energetic bodies as we intentionally engage in the vibrational world. In vibrational and energetic reality, boundaries are not like walls. Rather, energetic boundaries derive from making clear choices about how, when and where we are extending and retracting our vibrations outward and back into our energy body. Nothing is ever static at the level of vibration and energy. There is always some kind of movement and flow. Learning to consciously engage our power in the matrix of vibrations is an essential task in consciously creating the dream of our lives and the Earth.

After creating sacred space, vibrational work begins with feeling into your spiritual body and learning to clear energetic blocks, as well as restoring your energetic spirit body. We must be healthy before we can heal the world; and healing ourselves is healing the world. We are part of the body of the Earth, so any work that we do to bring ourselves back into vibrational alignment and completeness in any moment helps the Earth and all its people. Often, the specifics of our vibrational imprints as they manifest in our lives can represent a microcosm of larger issues that are going on around us and on the planet as a whole. Since we share and create stories together — all across the planet exists a web of dreams — our stories, our imbalances, our challenges and our healing mirror the stories of others.

EXERCISE: Immersion with the Four Directions

Purpose

You may experience people honoring the four directions at the beginning of ceremonies as a method for grounding. Often, I find honoring the four directions to be a time in a ceremony where participants from Western cultures seem unsure of or unengaged with why we are doing this. There are many reasons to engage in this practice: honoring spirits of the Earth and our elemental nature energies, ancestors, stories and so many more.

For many years, I intentionally avoided practices that seemed to have indigenous roots. The way of honoring the four directions seemed to me devoid of feeling and true engagement; the process seemed borrowed and unauthentic. I needed to find a way to feel into relationship with the directions, and through this seeking I found new ways of practicing rituals for the directions.

Description

I use two ways to help myself and others connect with the four directions in an embodied way. The first is to spend extended periods of time with each direction, speaking with the wind, the nature beings, the spirits that come from and reside there. I ask myself and others to invite the directions to open up and reveal themselves, always with great gratitude for anything that may come.

To begin, inside or outside, locate and face each direction. I begin with the north. Again, I am not trained in this by people, but by the Earth; I felt my way into the practice. If you subscribe to a specific belief system with the directions, start with whatever direction fits with your current practice. Sit facing each direction for an extended period of time. Whether on your own or in a group, this can be minutes, hours or a day. If you have a day for each direction, then you will begin to foster profound understanding of the directions. Since most of us don't often have a day to honor and connect with each direction on a regular basis, I recommend taking a length of time between 15 minutes and an hour. One way is to set aside a week to spend your spiritual time each day with a direction.

I get a very interesting reaction with groups when I set aside two hours of a workshop to be with the four directions. They are more used to five to 20 minutes at the most for any four-directions activity, so they often balk at this radical slowing down. In some cases, relating to the directions is the entire ceremony. As with most of the practices that bring us back into contact with our natural sensitivities, this simple commitment to slowing down reaps surprising realizations and rewards of expanded connection with the life-world.

There are two ways to expand this practice. The first is to imagine, or ask others to imagine, any significant nature beings or landmarks in each direction and reach out to them to ask questions, give gratitude and invite direction on how we can honor and bring healing through our relationships with them. In my bioregion, Lake Erie is most often the largest significant nature being to the north, so we start by speaking to the lake. At many of my retreat locations, we have an important river to the east. I also acknowledge any creeks, trees, glens or other beings in each direction in our immediate locale.

Another method to expand the practice of connecting with the directions is to imagine as you, and others, face each direction that you are reaching out with your light from your heart all the way around the Earth in a band of light until this beam connects to you again through your back. With a group, each person does this in the direction that they are facing. The result is the experience of a web of light originating from the circle and expanding around the body of the Earth in every direction.

EXERCISE: Clearing Sacred Space
Purpose

To support a practice of healing with vibrations, it is helpful to create vibrationally clear "zones." Many rituals that we take for granted in our religions and/or spiritual practices come from an unconscious (or conscious, but long-forgotten) sensitivity to supporting vibrational and consciousness shifts to support spiritual experience. Creating rituals to open our vibrational and energetic practices helps us to clear space to support our work to bring healing and transformation with light.

Description

Though each person's practice can be private and different, common practices that are used around the world are a good place to begin. Later in this book we will talk about the importance of music and dance to help raise vibrations, but for now I want to talk about some very simple ceremonial elements. Also, it can be easier to clear space and raise vibrations in peaceful nature settings, as these environments help us develop a sense of calm and bring us into a reverential state.

I use rocks to help balance and clear vibrational space in rituals. I used rocks for spiritual practice for many years without understanding what they provided. Through extensive practice, I now feel circles of stone as vortices of vibrationally cleared and open energy. Rocks in a circle can support our communication with the Divine because messages from elemental earth energies and spirit helpers are difficult to receive through our typically dense vibrational reality. It is a mystery that many cultures have known over time, that circles of rock and stone support our connection as gateways to other realms and shift our consciousness for perceptions of "other worlds." Also, circles that are drawn or created with other natural objects can support our spiritual awareness and development, as described in the Earth-connecting practices earlier in this book.

Other elements to add to your ritual are fire, smoke from burning herbs or incense and water. I have seen people use these in many religions and spiritual practices but didn't understand, until I started moving into deeper vibrational awareness, that fire, water and smoke clear vibrational space. Smoke truly does carry our prayers to heaven, and helps us listen to the wisdom that returns, by lightening vibrations so that communication can happen across the veils.

To begin my ceremonies, I arrange a circle of rocks small, large or very large, depending on the size of the area I have to work with and the way in which I want to work in the space. I may want to sit inside or outside of the mandala, sit on one position or move around the mandala. I follow my intuition and connect with the place to help me choose the size of the circle. I arrange my sacred stones and other beings and objects, start a fire if in a safe place outside (or use candles inside) and also make sure I have a bowl of water. I circle my body with some kind of smoke, imaging a cleansing of my circle. I found my own way to many of these practices, and only later pieced together why they are part of traditional religious practices in Western and many other cultures.

Again, it takes consistent practice to understand and embody the experience of these methods. You don't need to feel anything special for these ceremonies to work, and over time people often do begin to feel the shifts that these practices engender.

You can also clear space with singing, with drumming, using singing bowls, chimes and crystals for visualization. When you clear with sound or images, imagine a divine light coming down through the top of your head and through your heart into the sound or image, lighting it up. Then picture this light moving out in every direction, creating a center of clarity and peace in your ceremonial space.

EXERCISE: Opening Your Heart

Purpose

After creating sacred space, grounding and setting an overarching intention, the next step to increasing our vibrational awareness is to connect with our own light, which enters and exits through our heart-mind. Our heart is a center of experience, but also offers us a method of knowing and direction that can send messages of healing to our head/brain-mind.

When you begin a vibrational awareness practice, ideally you will be well prepared and present in your body from engaging in Earth-connected embodied practices. As we move fully into our own bodies, this enhances our recognition of the energy flows and vibrations present in our bodies. To begin this practice, we open the source of light in our own bodies, our heart centers.

Description

First, slow down — always slow down — so that you can feel your heart beating. Listen to your heart and feel the energy of the blood leaving your heart and moving throughout your body. As you focus on this movement, imagine that each beat of your heart is sending not just blood, but streams of light through your veins. Feel the light move from your heart to the surrounding areas of your body in concentric rings. Then, imagine someone you love. Feel the emotion of deep love that you have toward this person. Picture that love spreading out to the universe and coming back to you. Imagine that you are surrounded by a loving force that is holding you in a bright, white light all around you. Feel love from this force coming into your body, holding you, loving you exactly as you are, with no expectation.

You are complete and everything is right and at peace for you in the light of this love. Imagine now a beam of light emanating from this divine source of love and coming toward you. As this light reaches you, it suffuses your heart, which begins to grow and glow around your body with the force of the love. Your heart is now full, round, pulsating, softly yet brightly glowing with this love. Divine love has entered your chest and lit the candle of your spirit. You are now awake to the reality of the center of divine light that lives in your own body.

EXERCISE: Waking Up Your Energy Body: Creating Your Ball of Light

Purpose

This exercise helps you work with, feel, shift and clear vibrations in your energy body. At first, you may not feel anything. The great thing about vibrational work is that it's effective whether you feel it or not; it happens because of the creative power of thought forms and stories. In this exercise, you will envision a story of a ball of light moving through your body to help you see and feel your personal vibrational field.

This exercise is much like a "body scan," something you may have tried in the past. The goal is to wake up to your entire body; first its physical element, then emotional and energetic.

Description

To begin, find a comfortable, safe place to sit or lie down. With practice you'll be able to do this exercise anywhere, but for now give yourself quiet and privacy, if you can. And, remember that all vibrational work is enhanced and supported by direct grounding with the Earth. So if you can sit or lie down outside, with some part of your skin touching the Earth, that will make this exercise even more effective. It is helpful, but not necessary, to play relaxing, meditative music, preferably with no words, as music helps to shift our brainwaves for easier access to the imaginal realms.

Once you are comfortable and settled, gently place your hand on your belly and feel yourself breathe, five or ten times. When you feel in synch with your breath, imagine that each inhalation is sending your breath to a specific place in your body — right toes, right foot, right leg, so on — until you have imagined breathing into every part of your body. You can do this in even closer detail if you want to, such as breathing into each toe, then each part of your foot, ankle, calf etc.

Once you are breathing into your body, imagine that there is a ball of white light over your head, resting a few inches above and behind you. Imagine that this ball of light is the size of a medium-sized orange. Take time to let the image of this ball of light come into view for you. What is its temperature, its size? What is the surface like? Can you see through it? Is it glowing? Is the surface swirling or still? Is it circling or rotating, or just a solid stationary mass? There are no right answers to these questions. You are imagining this light, so it can be whatever you want it to be.

Once you are comfortable with holding this ball of light in your mind's eye, let it begin to move slowly up and down your spine. Imagine that it is softly drifting down your back against your spine. Not inside your body for now, but just touching your spine as it moves down your back to your tailbone. Let it rest against your tailbone briefly before moving back up your spine to above your head again. When you see this, imagine clearly in your mind that the ball of light is entering through the top of your head and moving throughout your entire body, in whatever order or way that you want it to. Do this exercise often to help you learn to imagine your body as energy.

When you are comfortable with the ball of light exercise, you can begin to clear space in your body. Feel in your body for any tension, pain, discomfort or illness. When you locate a block in your body's energy flow, feel into it and let it become a color, a temperature, a texture and/or a shape in whatever way that it presents for you. Move your ball of light to that place in your body, and imagine the ball of light surrounding it, not seeking to change anything but just to hold it in light just as you are. Acceptance of whatever is held in our energy bodies begins a process of transmutation by allowing our own healing processes to flow. It is releasing blocks through love, and light vibrations.

EXERCISE: Calling Your Spirit Back to You

Purpose

We put our spirit out to many things in the world. Issues and events in our own lives, in our families and our communities, as well as events and problems around the world, pull our energy. When we do spiritual work, it is important to call our spirits back to ourselves, at least for the moment. Other ways of expressing and understanding this concept include "leaving our worries at the door" or "being in the moment."

Calling our spirits back to us is more than this, though. It requires developing awareness of what issues are drawing our spiritual resources outside of us, whether good or bad. The parts of our lives that pull our spirit can sometimes be felt as tendrils reaching from our spirit bodies out into the world. To use all of our resources for any specific spiritual work, we need to call our spirit back to us as much as we can, even if only for a short time.

Description

Use the karmic eddy exercises to become aware of what is drawing your spirit into the world in general or most specifically at a given time. Recently, I am reliving old patterns of overly care-taking others. This is pulling a large amount of my physical and spiritual resources. I am actually giving my spirit body to others.

Sometimes this is a good thing to do, although we need to do it consciously or it will drain us. Sometimes I do this for other people's benefit, and sometimes to soothe myself or manage my own anxiety. Whatever the reasons, this is one area that at the moment I need to work on with my karmic eddy contemplations and when I am doing spiritual work.

When you prepare to call your spirit back to you, consider any old stories or patterns that are coming up in your life. These are often represented by repetitive thoughts or worries, or compulsions (one of mine is overworking). Other things that call my spirit right now are important to me and part of my sacred work: supporting my family through the death of an unexpected loved one; helping my children navigate the challenges of growing in difficult times; keeping my marriage healthy and strong over decades.

Good or bad, when we call our spirit back we use awareness and kindness with ourselves as our primary tools. We may not know all of the things that are pulling us, and we don't have to resolve or fix anything in the moment. Sometimes, we suddenly wake up to something that has been just behind our conscious awareness for quite some time. These things may require more attention in the moment as they can be accompanied by unexpected and intense feelings. These are important to tend to, and are often worth setting our plans aside for the time being.

Once you feel aware of what is calling your spirit, imagine a soft white light all around your body, and see or feel tendrils of this light connecting to each of the things that came up for you during your reflection. Imagine, for the time being, that you are releasing these tendrils and see this energy coming back into your light body. If you feel strongly that you need to keep any of these tendrils extended, let them be. Sometimes we are holding active connections with others that need to be kept and honored as part of a sacred duty. Sometimes we can't let something go just yet, even for a short time. With gentleness and patience, let yourself be where you are.

Once your tendrils are called back to you, feel your light body relax and expand with the renewed energy of your spirit returning. Sit with the feeling of completion and fullness for a few minutes.

The next chapter provides skills to engage, create and influence vibrational fields on personal and global levels, through the work of managing and shifting our karmic eddies. Moving into work with our own karmic eddies, it is important to understand that we are either sending or receiving in the vibrational realm. Years ago, due to my intense sensitivity to psychic phenomena — again, limited words — I learned to create a bubble around myself that would repel unwanted incoming vibrations, from other people, spirits, thought forms and the field of human consciousness in general.

Now I know that there is much more to do than walking around protecting myself, and that the idea of protecting myself creates the opposite effect by drawing my fears toward me. Instead of imagining myself as armored for battle with dark and malevolent forces, I now know that I can take an active role in healing and transforming the vibrational fields of other people and the world by sending them light. It seems too simple to be true, as our minds complicate and question us out of knowing our own power, but sending light and love to people, situations and the planet is a source and expression of this power.

Once enough of us are sending love and light into the vibrational field of human consciousness, we will transform the direction of Western culture and our planet. This is already happening on a huge scale globally and when I meet people doing this work we know one another immediately. While the people of the planet, and our shared grief and pain, often seem insurmountable, we must believe that the impact of one person vibrating to frequencies of love and divine light does truly change the world. This is happening now; this shift in consciousness is growing; we can join together to encourage this shift of consciousness worldwide and bring ourselves into a new story for the planetary era.

12

Karmic Eddies:
Personal Vibrational Healing

My spirit guides gifted me the concept of karmic eddies, a powerful metaphor for actively working with light in vibrational reality. My guides taught me that karmic eddies are certain places that I go to with my body-mind energy. An eddy in a river or stream is caused by rocks, or other formations, that hold water — swirly, still, sometimes fetid — in place instead of moving with the flow. My karmic eddies hold my life force. Sometimes these flows are integrated with my soul path, and sometimes they are blocking my spirit from moving forward. Certain eddies pull my energy from the more essential work of presence to the world in each moment and awareness of the stories that I create in each moment.

Some of my karmic eddies are older than others, but all of them keep parts of me in certain habitual places, some supportive, some limiting and hurtful to the "flow" of my life and spiritual growth. Many karmic eddies are made by our own choices, whether these are conscious or not. Some are programmed into our experience by higher beings to support our learning. All require attention and awareness to call our spirits back to us when needed to connect fully with the Earth, work in vibrational reality and vision through awake dreaming.

Karmic eddies are places of important learning. We move our life force into holding patterns along the stream of our river of life to attend to hurts, complexities, sacred missions and growth opportunities. Often, karmic eddies are unfinished business that we brought with us into this life, or things that happened to us that are out of our control. Sometimes they are memories that we bring from past lives, or that help us gain skills and grit for the tasks of a future life. Karmic eddies may bring us to places in time or out of time.

Often, even after completing the purpose of a karmic eddy, we return to them again and again, through memories, reflections, resentments, fears or repetitions of patterns and stories that form our identity. While karmic eddies have an important place in our development as souls, it is also important to learn to complete them and call the energy of these eddies back into the river of our lives.

EXERCISE: Karmic Eddy Mandala Drawing

Purpose

Many of our karmic eddies are out of our awareness, or such a usual part of our consciousness that we don't notice them. Drawing a mandala of the eddies in our lives can help us develop awareness of the places that pull our spirit. We use the ancient symbol of a circle to place our karmic eddies in a symbol that consciously or unconsciously brings attention to our place in the larger community of life and the cosmos. We use a circle to feel the balance or imbalance that karmic eddies bring to our lives.

Description

Begin by gathering art supplies to create a drawing. You will need paper and a pencil, pen, crayons, colored pencils, markers or paint. Keep it simple. This exercise is about increasing your self-awareness, so try to release any fears or pressure to make "art." Using simple materials may help you release expectations and return to a "child's mind" about your karmic eddy mandala.

To support this simplicity, I use children's Crayola markers or crayons and any piece of plain paper. You can also do this exercise on a page in your journal of on a piece of scrap paper. The karmic eddy mandala drawing is something to do again and again, as the currents of our lives are constantly shifting and changing. Remaining aware of our stories and patterns requires reassessing on a regular basis.

The task of creating a karmic eddy mandala is simple, while the realizations and feelings that emerge are often surprising and intense. Begin by drawing a circle on a piece of paper of any size. Draw symbols, images, words, or even scribbles and different colors that represent the karmic eddies in your life right now. When I do this exercise, I often use a spiral to represent each karmic eddy in my life. As I draw, the spirals might blend together or birth new spirals and offshoots. Your karmic eddies can be anywhere on the page in relation to the circle. Listen to your body and intuition as you choose situations to represent on the mandala. This is not a thinking exercise, but rather like free writing: let it flow. You can do it again and again, so there is no need to "get it right."

Begin to draw images or symbols of things in your life that feel like they take up space or pull your attention again and again. These can be good things or bad things, or somewhere in between. As you draw your karmic eddies, you can include past hurts that you return to often, or attempt to keep from happening again, such as small and large annoyances with family members, friends and co-workers. You can draw important memories from your past that influence your present and perceptions of your future, major traumas and the best moments that you can remember. You can also draw habits of worry about performance, place, work, body image and money.

Many of my karmic eddies are shared, perpetuated by the consciousness of our Western industrial culture (some examples include: money worries, body shame, fear for the environment, political anger, many "isms" and concerns for humanitarian crises and wars around the world). You might draw life themes: things that you think about or have feelings about again and again.

Cultivate loving kindness toward yourself as you increase recognition of the eddies and paths in the river of your life. Each represents important and sacred work during your time on Earth. You can decide when that work is done, and you can retrieve your spirit from these swirls of energy in your life whenever you are ready. Many of our karmic eddies express patterns of our communities and cultures.

As I (gently) identify and remind myself to swim out of my karmic eddies for another perspective, I find myself more often experiencing the open flow of a beautiful, soulful life. Swimming more freely in the river of life, I find more space each day for joy, gratitude and magic. As we bring awareness to, feel into and unravel our karmic eddies, we also do this work for the world. As we change our stories we foster new dreams for the Earth.

EXERCISE: Karmic Eddy Clearing

Purpose

A karmic eddy clearing is an artistic and imaginal meditation for clearing emotional blocks. This practice can provide respite and relief from habitual body-mind patterns. Clearing these patterns can increase healing and connection in our lives, and open fresh paths for us in many ways.

Some karmic eddies are old and ready to be released, some are areas where we are still working. Some karmic eddies are sticky and seductive and require that we return to work with them on a regular basis. Creating harmony with and among our karmic eddies allows us to sink with the "flow" of soul expressed as an integrated river of life source energy. My mind-body habit swirls are familiar: many so familiar that I am barely aware of them. Each is a place in which I have done important growth work.

Description

When you feel that your drawing from the previous exercise is complete, find a comfortable position for gazing softly at your karmic eddy drawing. Invite intuitive guidance using the "Opening Your Heart" Meditation from Chapter Eleven. Set an intention that you will connect with your karmic eddy drawing for healing. As you intuitively connect with your drawing, tune in to the sensations in your body that may show up in connection to certain karmic eddies that you've identified in your drawing.

Feel into the sensation in your body. If it helps, you can close your eyes and imagine that you're floating above your body to "see" the sensation. What does it look like, feel like? Does it have a color, a shape, a texture? Ask yourself if you may want to change it in any way. If you feel resistance to this, don't seek to make this change right now. Just be with the sensation. If you do feel ready to make a change, imagine a new color, temperature, shape, texture to this sensation and imagine this shift taking place.[67]

Clearing karmic eddies with people and in the world: A variant on the karmic eddy clearing is to use light to clear or transmute situations with specific people, or in the world, that are pulling or blocking your energy. I am grateful to the planetary guide, Joseph, for this exercise, which I've adapted somewhat over time.[68] Again, this doesn't mean that we block feelings that we have in relation to these situations. Instead, we suffuse them with light and bless them with an intention for the healing of the world. From there, it is not our responsibility to fix them or to manage our feelings, but to let our stories shift as the light that we bring transmutes these situations for and through us.

Often, we do this without sensing any immediate effect, accepting that our work may not show for many years to come. Interestingly, visualizing with light can influence situations across time, so that something might suddenly drastically change, as if we have gone backward in time to change the future.

To effect change with people and worries outside of your body, close your eyes and imagine the person, issue or situation appearing about an arm's length in front of your face. Visualize the details of the karmic eddy with as much detail as possible. Once you have a clear image, imagine divine light coming in as a bright beam through the top of your head and through your heart. Picture this beam of divine light suffusing the image of the karmic eddy. Paradoxically, we must do this practice while intentionally releasing any effort to fix or change a situation. Instead, bless it just as it is; make a prayer that all involved will be blessed by Great Spirit in this day. Then imagine the person, issue or situation suffused in this beam of divine heart light, becoming brighter and brighter until it is glowing in white light.

Continue to suffuse the image with light and notice any shifts or blocks that you may have. Our attachments to karmic eddies become abundantly clear during this exercise. If you are angry or very resistant, do your best, sending a blessing of love, and intention, or a prayer to protect them and bring them joy and to help them fulfill the goals of their spirit and soul in this life. If you are angry at a world leader or feel that someone with power in the world is bringing destruction or pain, you can do this same exercise. Imagine people or places in the world in great pain and send light from your heart and suffuse them with love and light. I know that this can seem like we are doing nothing when so much is wrong with the world, but you will find with practice that light healing shifts your own stories, which will begin to flow into the world in concentric circles of action.

I also send light to people who I love and feel no conflict with, to situations, and especially to my spirit helpers and to the Divine Spirit of the Universe every day. We are not separate from anyone or anything, and as we share our heart light with others, barriers we might not have been aware of fall away and we experience deeper intimacy.

Close this meditation by opening your eyes, wiggling your toes and tapping lightly on the top of your head. Return completely to the space that you are in and notice your surroundings. Close with gratitude to yourself and your guides for engaging in this important work. Expect some feelings to arise over the next days and weeks as the shift that you've initiated begins to take shape in your body and mind. If you feel overwhelmed at any point, ground to the Earth through your feet and let any strong emotions flow through your feet to the Earth.

Send Light to All Things

Sending light to all beings, to all people, to all great and beautiful things, as well as to all worries, traumas, horrors and fears, is a powerful healing practice that anyone can do. As you send heart light to your body, your feelings, your thoughts, so too can you send light to people, places and situations all over the world.

This action may seem too simple to work, but amazing results can come from this practice. I have had entrenched conflicts and hurts transform in very unexpected ways from using this practice, and while it doesn't seem to instantly change the world, primarily because of the limitations of our own collective beliefs, this practice does bring profound healing in ways that we often don't understand. If we do this regularly, perceptions and feelings about ongoing struggles in our communities and the world begin to change.

In any moment, as often as we can remember, we can open a door in our heart to bring light into the world. In any given moment, imagine a ball of light moving softly from your heart and going into the heart of another person, a place or a situation. On my best days, I do this with every person I encounter. Walls fall down, people open up, feelings are shared, people feel seen. This can be very hard to do if I am distracted, angry, rushed or pulled into my own experience in any number of other everyday ways. Yet inevitably, giving love changes us and the world even in our worst moments and in our greatest pain.

For one day, try to see everyone and everything surrounded with heart light. This is a very quick way to find out how unconscious we can be, how easy it is to shift our reality and truly impact everything around us.

Part 4

Dream-Connecting Practices

13

Dream-Connecting: Creating New Stories in Vibrational Reality

Dream-connecting is the Earth Spirit Dreaming gateway to the spirit realms — the final step on the path to reconnecting with the spirit helpers of this planet and beyond. At this pivotal time in human history, the spirit helpers of Earth, our ancestors in the spirit realms and what we might call "angels," are waiting for us to ask for help. They are ready to show us the way to re-illuminate our lives and to bring us into alignment with the original dream of Gaia. These spirit helpers surround our planet, attempting in every moment to break through the weight and heaviness that surrounds us, created by the beliefs and thought patterns that smother our minds in heavy padding. As our spirit helpers reach out to us, it is as if we are wrapped in blankets, unable to feel them; wearing blindfolds, unable to see the path that they are showing; our ears stuffed with cotton, unable to hear their guidance and wisdom. It is time to enliven our spiritual sensitivities and to access the vibrational frequencies needed to communicate with our spirit helpers. The Earth Spirit Dreaming practices all lead to this pivotal task of dreaming our way back to our spirit helpers, our ancestors, the elemental nature spirits and the Divine Spirit of the Universe; now is the time to reconnect fully with our genetic inheritance of embodied spiritual realization.

This chapter begins the journey toward the culmination of the two previous parts of the Earth Spirit Dreaming method. Dreaming practices guide readers to bring forth the Earth and Spirit intelligence that is now available through newly opened natural senses. From this doorway of dawning awareness, dream-connecting rituals help us enter the symbolic and imaginal realms of experience. Dreaming, in the context of this method, can be understood as a form of visioning and co-creating the world. Through the dream-connecting practices, we relate to the imaginal realms in ways that are often limited by a focus on conceptual thinking. Through conscious dreaming, we shift our lives and the world from a state of clarity that comes from our grounding in our own embeddedness within in the Earth community. Through this process, we rediscover the mystery and deep magic surrounding us in every moment of life.

Dreaming as Co-Creation

The process of dreaming into a healing story for humans and the planet originates in our imagination. We are profoundly creative beings and what we see and feel in our mind-heart-bodies is what we create in the world. This understanding of our role in the co-creation of reality does not fit with currently accepted notions of an objective reality "out there." For a conceptual schema to help our minds release into this experience, we can rely on the perspective of scientists who support a holistic and participatory understanding of reality. One example is Ervin Laszlo's view of the expression of the two realms of reality, the inner subjective and the outer objective. Laszlo identifies consciousness as the "internal aspect" of the connectivity among systems.[69]

Ontologically, in a relational view of reality neither outer nor inner experience holds more merit than the other. Access to the spiritual realms through the gateways of our inner selves is no less "real" than the shared reality of an outer, objective world. Communities that honor the internal relationship to the "dream" realms share the experience of illuminated and magical experience in the outer "objective" world as well. As Laszlo elucidates in his book, *The Systems View of the World: A Holistic Vision for our Time*, our imaginations are a subjective experience of the interwoven systems of life and the cosmos:

> The phenomenon of mind is neither an intrusion into the cosmos from some outside agency, nor the emergence of something out of nothing. Mind is but the internal aspect of the connectivity of systems within the matrix. It is there as a possibility within

> *the undifferentiated continuum, and evolves into more explicit forms as the matrix differentiates into relatively discrete, self-maintaining systems. The mind as knower is continuous with the rest of the universe as known. Hence in this metaphysics there is no gap between subject and object.*[70]

The Earth- and Spirit-connecting practices of the previous chapters are intentionally oriented toward finding integration with the more-than-human world. The lens of creative thoughts and imagination is then interconnected with the dream of Earth and cosmos, through which we become mindful of other beings in the fabric of consciousness through relationship with vibrational reality.

Through shamanic experience, the result of portals into vibrational reality, we come to relate to beings that we know in our hearts are "real": elemental nature energies, ancestors and spirit helpers, among others. In relationship and authentic communion with these beings our new dreams of reality are kindled. From this place of nested participation, the lens of our primal creativity opens onto a landscape of shared abundance and rejuvenation embedded within an ethic of care for the Earth and all of life.

Visioning for healing begins from our heart-minds; the dreams that we bring into the world are drawn directly from what we think and experience in each moment. Experience of separation creates stories and dreams of anger, fear, anxiety and greed; an experience of relationship creates stories of interrelatedness, love and a blended flow with the processes of life. Tragic and painful things happen in the world; loss and grief are part of the processes of life. Our co-creation comes from how we greet these moments. Owning our co-creation in every moment does not mean that we are in charge of everything that happens, but rather that we become aware of our profound impact in the world by how we relate to all that happens in the world.

It is both scary and empowering to discover on a visceral level that we are, in every moment and through every conscious or unconscious thought, engaged in creating the world. We evolved with power, to transform and illuminate all happenings and experiences by greeting them with open hearts. Dreaming our experience from a place of conscious and authentic openheartedness is joyful, exhilarating, raw and wild. This is the condition of "awake" humans on Earth; we are swimming in the wild flow and emergent spontaneity of relationships; the interwoven vibrational reality of the universe.

Vibrational Experience in Western Cultures

As the orientation of Western culture is grounded in disconnection, the connection with "all our relations" gives us new information to reach beyond the limits of our current abilities to understand or believe. Moving into contact with elemental nature energies, seeking engagement with spirit helpers and speaking and listening to the Earth, we are directed to see new possibilities. In this new world of participatory reality and belief structures, acknowledging co-creation through dreaming in the vibrational realm is central to engaging healing for the Earth.

In the Cartesian worldview, substance is separate from process, self from other and thought from feeling. A systems perspective, conversely, sees what appear to be separate, "self-existent" entities as mutually constitutive.[71] Joanna Macy, a systems thinker, refers to the image of nerve cells in a neural net to symbolize the nature of information flows. This image is suggestive of an important systems insight: mind is not separate from nature, but rather is ubiquitous in the "circuitry" of the flow of information. This flow takes place at the level of vibrations, both the originator of and background "field" of our shared realities.

In the history of Western thought, there are many attempts to grapple with numinous experience within the limits of truth as ideas in the context of objective reality. Immanuel Kant, in his first *Critique*, takes pains to emphasize that "Transcendental and transcendent are not interchangeable terms ..." [72] Transcendent means beyond the limits of experience, while transcendental means necessary conditions of experience. American transcendentalist Ralph Waldo Emerson restates Kant's view by suggesting that transcendent could mean beyond the *usual* limits of experience. Emerson's hope, channeling some of the romantic thinkers who maintained the possibility of knowing beyond reason in the history of Western thought (Goethe, Shelling, Swedenborg, Coleridge, Blake, Hugo), is to encourage others to access revelatory experiences that derive from a profound sympathy with the natural world.

Earthly American philosopher Charles S. Peirce describes his own experiences that exist "beyond reason" as connecting to a higher principle in the universe simply through the act of allowing his mind to open freely for long periods of time. He argues that, given the opportunity, any mind will find its way to oneness with the universe through the mind's natural capability of accessing these higher spheres. For Emerson, the experience of "beyond" came from these sympathetic experiences in nature as an entrée to the imaginal realms of experience. When the perceptual bridge that created the experience of unity/correspondence could be crossed, other experiences, sensations, sense of time and space, and other beings were encountered.

The visionary nun, Hildegard of Bingen, offered the Western world visions into vibrational reality through numinous experience long before the Enlightenment closed the door on these kinds of truths. As can be found throughout Western thought and traditional religions, the wisdom of the mystics always returns to the fabric of "spirit" underpinning reality; a divine force that is mysterious, always shifting and changing, somehow knowable, but never to be fully understood. Cynthia Overweg, in her article "Hildegard of Bingen: The Nun Who Loved the Earth," illuminates Hildegard's understanding of an intimate knowing and love of nature as being the gateway to the underlying matrix of the cosmos:

> *In Hildegard's worldview, a beam of sunlight, the fragrance of a flower, or the graceful movement of a swan were all participants in the holy chorus of creation. To be out of sync with the beauty and fecundity of nature is to deny the divine force which enlivens body and soul. She called this force* **viriditas**, *using the Latin word for "greenness."*

She envisioned this "greening power" as a force that continually nourishes the earth and all its creatures. For Hildegard, the color green symbolized nature's vibrancy, ripening, and eternal becoming. She made it clear that we are not separate from nature, but an intimate part of it. When she observed the wonder and splendor of nature, she saw a divine underpinning which sustained not only the earth, but the cosmos. "Creation is the song of God," she said.[73]

Nature as a Gateway to the Vibrational Matrix of Life

As we approach the gateway to the vibrational realm — the place of stories, symbols, spirit and "magic" — we can help ourselves across the threshold by soothing our questioning minds with science. To create a story of deep connection, we have to talk our rational minds into why these states of being are possible. Along with systems theory, as used by Laszlo, Macy and other important holistic thinkers, quantum theory is another avenue.

In an interview published in *The Holographic Paradigm and Other Paradoxes*,[74] David Bohm argues that the challenge for the "individual locus of consciousness" is to provide the condition that allows the universal force to awaken the participatory experience.[75] In Bohm's case, this would be a perception of the implicate order — another term for vibrational reality — made manifest through an awakened experience of the explicate world. The result, for Bohm, is not knowledge in a Kantian sense, but direct non-dual awareness. Bohm argues that non-dual awareness causes the suspension of Kant's categories of reason, and of three-dimensional space-time.[76]

In Bohm's view, this cessation of consciousness as "the knower" then allows the noumenal intelligence to operate directly through the individual. This is another way of understanding the role of the dreamer as co-creator through conscious engagement with noumenal intelligence, the consciousness of the cosmos as expressed in the vibrational matrix that underlies all of life.

In his book, *The Visionary Window: A Quantum Physicist's Guide to Enlightenment*, Amit Goswami describes quantum mechanics as a way to understand experiences that seem to abide "beyond reason."[77] He suggests that there exists in all of us a quantum self; a part of us that is accessible beyond the limits of what we understand as shared physical reality. He refers to both the experience of quantum reality and the notion of the quantum self: "One spectacular aspect of any quantum mechanics is the possibility of nonlocal correlation — parts of a system that are separated by distance dancing in phase in a coordinated, coherent fashion."[78] And later in the book, Goswami continues with the same idea, suggesting that "as we fall into a quantum self we become privy to a nonlocal window of memories — past, present and future." [79]

Emerson experienced moments of "transcendent" awareness, or highly sympathetic states that he believed were required for vision, rather than mere observation, to occur. The experience that brought me into contact and knowing of vibrational perception came, as with Emerson, through extensive meditation and reflection in nature. As I watched the world, and the higher consciousness of my "watcher" watched me watching, the edges of "object reality" melted away into something else. As I've worked as an energy healer and shamanic practitioner it is my supposition that we can sense, experience and create at the level of vibrational reality, known to physicists as the level of the quanta: a non-local subsystem of reality that spreads across vast distances and time, and is essentially unconceivable and unobservable without taking into account the impact of the observer. Yet again, we find in these moments that we can relate with life beyond the limits of cognition.

Along with philosophers, scientists and thinkers of all kinds in Western thought, psychologists struggle to fit notions of the self and the psyche into objective and "reasonable" terms. Analytic philosopher W.V.O. Quine brilliantly captures the experience of reaching the edges of reality as it can be quantified with concepts in his essay, "Ontological Relativity."[80] Quine postulates the image of a flat surface with frayed edges to denote the flat map of Western knowledge of the world. These edges are constantly being rewoven and remade but are always tearing and rupturing as we struggle to stretch with reason and concepts to where we perceive that something exists, but to where the mind alone cannot travel.

Carl G. Jung, who himself grappled to understand his encounters with spirit helpers through his deep immersion into imaginal and symbolic experience, describes experience at the edges of conceptual reality in the reflections and art of *The Red Book*.[81] Jung felt and perceived the underlying fabric of something larger that human reason, creating a psychological metaphysics of the collective unconscious to express his realization.

Jung's commitment to working with mandalas both represented and took his awareness beyond the edges of rational experience, where he knew something existed and could be known, but only through non-scientific and non-rational methods. His sensitivities to the underlying matrix of the cosmos eventually led him into a dark night of the soul — a spiritual emergency, emotional breakdown, or a psychotic episode, depending on your orientation — a typical initiation experience of shamanic personalities. Though I had many spiritual emergencies through my teens and twenties, it was hearing trees talking and dreaming of messages from recently deceased family members that began a series of initiations that I only understood in retrospect. I hold these times with profound respect for what they wrought in my soul, forging me into a new vessel of perception through inner and outer fires that I might not choose to live through again. Yet, these are the crucibles that make us seers, spiritually awake and prepared to be with the intensities of life in all her forms.

In *The Red Book*, Jung works through the deep questioning of his soul, as he slips outside of this world and into others. He keeps a record of his visions and encounters through writing and art work. *The Red Book* is a journal through Jung's process of moving beyond reason into the wholly non-rational, even up to and including the "psychotic" and arguably shamanic experience of other beings. This is Jung's memoir of a shamanic awakening. The release of linear reality into the realms of magic. He identifies early in the book that this is happening to him because he has avoided the depths and longings of his own soul.

Allowing himself to fall fully into the reality of his dreams, Jung digs further into the life of his soul, questioning all assumptions of his own cultural and religious heritage. In his words, considering the essence of God, he dreams of an old man, who he calls a prophet. A black serpent is on the ground before him, and a beautiful blind maiden steps out of a door of a house with columns. He is eventually brought across a threshold into other worlds:[82]

> *The old man waves to me and I follow him to the house ... Darkness reigns inside of the house. We are in a high hall with glittering walls. A bright stone the color of water lies in the background. As I look into its reflection, the images of Eve, the tree, and the serpent appear to me. After this I catch sight of Odysseus and his journey on the high seas. Suddenly a door opens on the right, onto a garden full of bright sunshine. We step outside and the old man says to me, "Do you know where you are?"* [83]

Magic, Imagination, and the Quantum Self

Some of the energies, sensations and experiences that arise through a return to knowledge and experience in vibrational reality often feel ancient and dramatically wild. These can include fundamentally non-linear incidents and encounters that feel outside of time, or existing in radically unusual and reordered experiences of time and space. Moving beyond the mechanistic-Cartesian and industrial belief systems, we find our way to knowing beyond time and space as many of us know it. We discover that communication is possible across immense distances, and the edges of "objective" shared reality are porous and fluid. We merge into quantum reality, sense the holotropic nature of the cosmos, experience that each part is contained in the whole. We discover that we are in the whole and that the whole is in us; the universe seems to reside in a starry sky accessible by falling through and into the gateway of our own hearts.

When we step beyond the limits of reason, it is our imagination that becomes the path to shamanic experience. At first, and often after, we may doubt ourselves and wonder if we are "crazy." Perception and events are beyond synchronicity and can only be described as magical. A kind of meta-synchronicity draws us into a vast network of consciousness that we now know is there, but that we can no longer fully understand or conceptualize to its outer reaches. We only know that we are nodes on a vast web; we are distinct yet fully merged with miraculous interwoven rivers of vibrations. I now realize that while we cannot understand why or how vibrational reality exists, we can foster relationships within vibrational reality. While the limits of our human minds cannot conceive this vast matrix of light, our hearts can access and interact with vibrational reality through love.

Shamanic practitioner and teacher Sandra Ingerman emphasizes the importance of imagination to access the energy fields of the shaman: "Imagination is another key element in performing the miracle of transmutation. We must be able to envision an environment that is pure and clean and which supports all of life. With the power of imagination, we have the ability to sculpt the world we live in."[84]

As Ingerman, and so many others, remind us, we are "dreaming the wrong dream." We believe that we are separate from nature; thus we make it so through our thoughts, actions and inherent creative nature as light beings. Our own imaginations are so atrophied through our culture, and lack of connection with Earth and Spirit, that the visions we come up with from our place of separation are anemic at best, and dangerous and destructive at worst. Ingerman continues; "These illusions are seeds that grow into plants of fear, anger, hate, despair, and darkness. We need a new dream to create a new earth."[85]

The imaginal realms are where we leave the boundaries of reason and concepts and enter into symbolic reality. Shamanic experience, the place of visioning, intersects with the journey of science into the underpinnings of life and the heart of the cosmos, discovering knowing beyond the limits of innate mental structures, seen in the ability to become aware of the structures themselves.

In *An Encyclopedia of Shamanism*,[86] Christina Pratt captures the journey of Western science to find our way back to the fundamental nature of reality; a world of vibrations, visions, dreams, stories and the matrix of cosmic consciousness:

> We live in interesting times. Our foremost scientists, to whom we have given the task of explaining the material nature of our universe, are now describing a universe that the shamans have been describing for thousands of years. The scientists have arrived there through fact and experimentation and the shamans through their experiences in altered states of consciousness. We are coming full circle. It is as if the shamans have stood still and the developed world has gone around the circle the long way, through rigorous scientific exploration, and arrive where humanity started, in the shaman's universe.[87]

River Light

In my journey, I walk up a hill and cross a threshold overlooking the ocean. Above me are stairs leading to the "higher worlds." Standing on a hill, I feel a breeze as I look over the breathing waves and feel the pattern of the water currents, the blood of the Earth, moving across the globe, lifting into the atmosphere to fall again into rivers and streams and back to the pulsing Mother Ocean, tugged and released by the pull of the moon. Ocean reaches out to me and I feel her veins stretch into the mountains, fingers reaching across time to the sky to pull the waters into her belly, always reaching and receiving. Always breathing. This is a place that I often visit to meet my spirit sister; a caring friend and helper and a sister from a past or future life. Now, she looks down on me from her gazebo of light floating above the white beach.

I remember a long-forgotten waking dream of feeling my body as an ancient woman, running through the trees. Fast, strong, leather wrapped around the sinew of my arms; I know that I was this woman, very long ago. I know that my role in my village was to live with and relate to the river, hearing and feeling her strength and story interwoven with the dreams of my people.

As I stand above the ocean in my journey, one half of my body becomes this woman, dark hair, brown skin deeply weathered, while the other reaches into a past and future self that channels the dancing light on the water and knows that within the moving waters is my access to the consciousness of the Earth and cosmos. River is my spirit sister, and my spirit self is able to wield the light from all rivers. I feel the two faces from a dream come together. I am River Light; this is my power, my mission, my work for the world in this lifetime.

14

Sacred Rituals: Pathways to Re-Dreaming the World

Through rituals, we encounter the Divine Mystery, and journey to the inner core of human consciousness. Rituals are basic expressions of humanity as we move through the complexities and challenges of life. They express reverence and intention and create a sanctuary of presence to connect with an underlying shared awe of moments in life that are the most essential yet the hardest to control and understand. Rituals mark shared human experiences across cultures and throughout time: birth, death, marriage, growing up, marking the seasons, honoring our stories of creation and the rhythms and patterns of nature as well as cosmic and divine spirals of being.

Many of us sense when we are experiencing a ritual as they share common elements: shared meaning-making among community members, a specific order of ceremony, repetition of beliefs, prayers, sacred stories and objects, laments, honoring life cycles, and often elements of smoke such as incense, the burning of herbs, candle lighting and fire. Rituals are often held in places that are sacred to the culture in which they are embedded, and take place in those locations again and again, imbuing these sites with immense and readily felt imprints of the sacred. Sacraments vary widely by culture and tradition but share the role of expressing the fundamental message of cultural belief systems through ceremonial repetition. Sacraments exemplify essential beliefs and tenets of a religion and/or spiritual tradition. All rituals also contain sacred creativity through a variety of art forms: music, dancing, visual art, beautiful and awe-inspiring clothing of many kinds and, in many cultures, body painting and mask making to represent spirits and beings from nature that are revered. Rituals in any tradition tell the great stories and myths that capture the movement through struggle to power and strength for the people. Rituals all connect us to the feeling that we are part of something larger than ourselves, and that this connection with something larger gives meaning and some element of safety to our lives and communities.

As a convert from Christianity to Judaism, and a purveyor of eco-spiritual traditions across cultures, I've noticed that many traditional rituals, among many cultures, include elements that create entrainment among participants and can also encourage trance states, either light or intense. These actions change brainwaves, moving participants into shifts of consciousness, often so subtle that people don't realize it's happening. They may just feel a "connection," a surge of feeling or fluctuation in the space.

For many Christians, the primary sacrament is communion, which uses bread and wine to represent the body and blood of Christ. This sacrament expresses the central belief of Christianity, that Jesus died for our sins. In the Jewish tradition, the central sacrament is the Torah, and the rituals of the Torah service culminate in taking the Torah from the ark in a very sacred way and reading from it with great reverence. The Torah captures many beliefs of the Jewish people, central among them that while their temple was destroyed over 2,000 years ago, and they were expelled from their holy land, the people will continue to survive because they carry their stories and traditions with them in the form of the Torah.

All religious traditions have sacred actions and beliefs that can seem implausible, or even outlandish, to outsiders, but are very normal to lifetime adherents. I'll use my own experience with Judaism as a primary example, as my move from one religion to another heightened for me the elements of rituals that in Christianity, which I grew up in, are the norm for me. In Judaism, I noticed right away traditions that seemed obviously connected to indigenous practices at some point and that directly encouraged shifts in consciousness: the long periods of chanting and rocking while praying (davening), wrapping of the arms seven time in thick bands of leather (tefillin) and blowing large sheep horns in a variety of rhythms (shofar). Jews also shake four species of sacred plants while honoring the four directions during the holiday of Sukkot.

It is just the same in any religion, as my Jewish friends and family remark about the seemingly bizarre beliefs of Easter, the most important Christian holiday. It seems incredibly strange to most of them that anyone could believe that Jesus was crucified, died, was buried, went to hell to face Satan, then rose from the dead and, as God in human form, then ascended into heaven, essentially leaving Earth without dying. This seems nonsensical to outsiders, yet can inspire Christians and move them to the depths of their souls. Everything that I've described can be understood in a shamanic context, and undoubtedly harkens back to a time when experiences that we now call shamanic existed in the realm of normal, sacred occurrences.

Western religious traditions all maintain elements that are shamanic in some way. Most of these "magical" elements in more progressive religious groups are now considered myths, and things that couldn't have really happened. In the Hebrew Bible, some examples of shamanic experience are Moses speaking with a burning bush, miracles of healing, bursts and flashes of divine light, direct honoring and communication with ancestors and angels, great prophetic and guiding dreams and visions, and so many more.

In the New Testament, these shamanic elements include a belief in particular spiritual gifts, "given by the Holy Spirit," most identified by the Apostle Paul. A few of these gifts, as listed in 1 Corinthians 12: 8—10, include: the gift of healing, miracle, prophecy and praying in tongues. And, the story of Jesus is essentially shamanic: he was a divine being, a part of God, that overcame death, moved between worlds to encounter different spirits and faced the greatest malevolent spirit on Earth, Satan, returning with a great healing for the people by vanquishing the most negative consciousness known to humankind, just as the great shamans and medicine people move into the spirit realms to face the darkest elements in individual lives and communities, and to release the power and influence of this darkness and these destructive forces.

In Earth Spirit Dreaming, and in general as Westerners finding our way back to individual connection with direct revelation, and a religious orientation that honors the Earth, there is a search for sacraments and new kinds of rituals that hold the central tenets of the emerging story of

Earth-care. These central tenets include the truths of visionary environmental thought: that everything is connected, that Earth is sacred and that we can each speak directly with helping spirits, elemental nature energies and ancestors. Further, visionary environmental thought assumes that we can each experience revelatory and numinous states.

All of these aspects of Earth-honoring rituals can be found buried deeply — or quite close to the surface — in traditional Western religions, and there are large swaths of religious communities across the Abrahamic traditions that are seeking and activating the Earth- and Spirit-connecting elements for healing the environment and our connection with nature within the sacred texts and structures of these religions.[88]

The best rituals of any tradition take us beyond the limits of our minds, into collective knowing, and utilize many means to do this. They tap into our senses and powerful emotions and bring us into contact with our ancestors, our angels, the cosmos and the Divine, who wait to receive us as we float and move among the stars within and without. Step by step, we move beyond the limits of our minds into the Divine Mystery.

Our heart-minds take us where our brain-minds cannot go. Soon our heart-minds instruct our brain-minds, instead of the other way around, and we are making the world anew through the yearnings of our soul and the working of our spirits. It is through creating rituals for re-dreaming the world that the Earth Spirit Dreaming three-step method comes into full fruition. The form of these three steps comes together in rituals that support creative visioning. Carefully prepared rituals activate visioning in alignment with the original dream of the Earth, and the consciousness of a new story emerging among people on the Earth at this time.

Western Earth-Honoring Sacraments

One of the most complicated aspects of the emergence of re-indigenized spiritual rituals is developing common sacraments. Some movements of eco-spirituality in the West connect with and modify pre-monotheistic religions, such as goddess and Gaia spirituality, adoption of Native American beliefs and practices and learning, the indigenous religions of genetic places of origin, such as Wicca, Druids, a variety of northern European shamanic traditions and a return to African tribal traditions. Sometimes Westerners seek the ancient indigenous religious practice of their own lineage, but just as often, or more often, we seek traditions from other lineages, often causing conflict and suffering along the way. Re-indigenizing is a messy and sometimes distressing process of exploring, learning and often appropriating indigenous traditions. I firmly believe that Westerners can find their own indigenous ceremonies and traditions by muddling through together, relearning to speak to and listen to the Earth and to move in the spirit realms, and to process and grow from these experiences in community. We are in a mess of confusion and separation, and it will be messy finding our way out.

I deeply honor the connection that Western people find in ancient Earth-honoring religions by seeking the indigenous cultures of their own places of origin. I believe that our ancestral memories and spiritual senses are catalyzed by contact with religious forms and locales that supported our evolution in specific areas. Yet, I also believe that there is value in creating rituals and sacraments that activate who we have become through the journey of enlightenment and the immersion in reason and science, and that emerge from connection with the land wherever we find ourselves.

Still, we need specific sacraments to represent developing and current experiences of our own new story and shifting consciousness. These sacraments must capture the great pain and challenge that we face: the desecration and destruction of the Earth. They must represent the new stories that capture our abilities and power to overcome the myriad tragedies that surround us and that are the result of human choices and actions. Whether or not we integrate and find them within traditional Western religions, we need pageantry, music, ritual orders and specific ceremonies that guide us again and again into the orientation of consciousness and actions that inspire us to face these challenges and take action for the Earth. I'm not suggesting that we are creating a new religion, but we are seeking to foster a spiritual orientation that can support a profound shift in perception and beliefs and create and maintain new (and ancient) practices for a healing that can only come through re-indigenizing. Deep ecologist and shamanic guide, Bill Pfeiffer, captures this idea beautifully in his book, *Wild Earth, Wild Soul: A Manual for an Ecstatic Culture*:

> *One of the misunderstandings that can arise in coming upon a book with such an ambitious title is that it is attempting to get all people to adopt the same cultural forms, and to do so en masse. This is not the case.*
>
> *The invitation here is to allow nature and direct experience to determine what kind of Earth-honoring culture is best suited for a particular community. There is a place for everyone in helping to sculpt a diversity of cultures where the health of the land and the people is primary.*[89]

I believe that these new ways of knowing and being can fit into any religious tradition that people already practice. I have seen many examples of how this is done, many of them chronicled in important works capturing Western religious return to Earth, such as the book *This Sacred Earth*.[90] We do not have to abandon who we are, but transform how we believe and engage at the threshold of the Great Mystery, and modify how we understand our relationship with the Earth and the Divine.

For Earth Spirit Dreaming rituals, there are many options for ritual objects. The "sacraments" that the ritual objects represent capture the central tenets of visionary environmental thought and experience: everything is connected, the Earth is sacred; we can experience Earth in new ways that change our consciousness, spiritual awareness in Earth-honoring ways and new stories of action for the Earth and new ways of living in balance with the Earth. So, sacraments for Earth Spirit Dreaming begin with things that represent and bring forth the essential elements and beings of the Earth stories, songs, art and dance that honor the Earth; ritual orders that mark the seasons and rhythms of nature; ritual elements that honor specific bioregions.

Creating Rituals for Earth Spirit Dreaming

Separating visioning practices into individual exercises is challenging, and somewhat misleading. Many of these practices blend together in intuitive creative moments. Really, the delineation is only required to reteach our minds to let go. Everything that we need to vision is readily available. We need only to coax our minds to release the conceptual limitations so convincingly taught to us through Western civilization. While many of these practices flow easily into one another, I break them up to allow a slow opening of the mind on a comfortable linear path into imaginal senses and skills.

Before doing any of the dreaming practices, it is important to first move through Earth- and Spirit-connecting practices from previous chapters. Choose as many as you like, but at least one, from each section to prepare yourself before engaging in visioning practices. By now, you may have settled on Earth and Spirit practices that are the most comfortable for you; if so, use the practices that you like best. Do them in order, and always do each step, even if you only have a short amount of time to spend on each one. If you are short of time, focus on preparation and connection with the Earth and Spirit realms; the images you receive in the visioning process will expand through more grounding and clarity of intention.

The Order of Rituals

In any Earth Spirit Dreaming ritual, the following steps, done in order, will prepare you for clear vibrational and visioning work. Rituals can be long and complex, short and simple, or anything in between. Over time, you will find your way into the practices and rituals that work best for you. Until you are able to know and feel your way through shamanic experience, it is important, at the minimum, to always include the following steps:

1. Begin with gratitude
2. Set an overall intention by praying that your ritual and visioning will be for the healing of the world
3. Create sacred space: assemble your altar

4. Ground to the Earth
5. Connect with spirit helpers: call in your light guides
6. Set a clear intention for the visioning practice
7. Do your visioning practice
8. Receive and reflect
9. End with gratitude

For any visioning process, begin by giving gratitude and setting a clear intention. I always bask in gratitude at the start of any ritual. This does so much to welcome the helping spirits, invite the Earth beings and energies to support your work and raise the vibrations to connect all that you do with the Divine Spirit of the Universe. I count blessings as much and as many as I am able. I sing songs of thanks and gratitude. Then, I always ask that my work in this ritual, and in my life, will bring my life into alignment for the healing of the world.

That is my prayer and it works wonders. You can journey to find your own prayer and/or spirit songs. I have many spirit songs that are given to me, and that I give as gifts to my spirit helpers and to the Earth. This one prayer — that all that I do will be in alignment for the healing of the world — is central to everything right, in the highest spiritual sense, that happens in my life. Feel free to make it your prayer as well. It was a gift to me from the light guides of the planet, and I gift it to you with gratitude and blessings for your unfolding spiritual mission.

My prayer:

> *"Divine Spirit and Creator of the Universe, all of my helping spirits and the light guides of the planet, I ask that you bring my life into alignment for the healing of the world. I ask that you move through me so that all that I do will bring light and healing to the world."*

I always ask that my rituals and visions be led by the light guides of the planet or my helping spirits. I always ask that my visioning will bring healing. I ask that my life and work will fulfill my spiritual mission on the planet, release blocks, open channels of love. I ask that I will be led and supported to lead others to know the light guides of the planet. I often ask my helping spirits for guidance in setting my intentions, rather than limiting my visualization with my own, separate understanding.

After years of prayer and spiritual work, I now know that the spiritual possibilities of my life tend to be so much more than I could ever imagine or hope for myself. We often feel anxious and want what we want in the moment, which is part of the human condition on the planet. It's normal to feel this way. Often, there is something that we can't quite see, or that we only feel an inkling of, that would actually do more to progress our own healing and spiritual development than what we can think of or allow ourselves to want in the current situations in our lives. Reaching with intention into the unknown requires trust and surrender to higher consciousness, and the light beings that guide and support us on this journey. Asking for support from our helping spirits as often as possible is the best way forward in all things.

EXERCISE: Gather Your Medicine

Purpose

When we begin a shamanic dreaming practice, we gather "medicine" from the Earth spirits, the helping spirits and the ancestors. Gathering items for your own altar will help you more quickly bring your senses into the states required to access other realms by acting as cues to help you reach altered states more quickly. These items also become charged up with our gratitude and connection to beautiful entities that guide us on our path into the magical realms. Many items on our altar bring their own power, as well as representing moments of gratitude and connection, and special messages and openings.

Description

As you commit to a dreaming practice, create a "medicine basket" of things to build your altar whenever you hold your ceremonies, for yourself or with others. The simplest basket or bag of things will include all of the elements: earth, air, fire and water. Your sacred stones, from the exercise in Chapter Six, are an excellent way to bring in the earth. Also include candles: small votive candles travel well. Air is what we are always breathing and is also seen when we burn herbs and plants to honor their spirits and bring in the wisdom of these particular plants. I include a bowl for filling with water on your altar. Include one or more objects that are sacred to you and that bring you positive feelings, connect you to your ancestors and/or remind you of special experiences that bring forward heightened feelings of connection. Also, choose a piece of cloth that is beautiful to you that you can lay down wherever you are to build your altar.

When you place your medicine items into an arrangement for your ceremony, hold this as a sacred act of reverence. Feel the essence and beauty of each item and the energy of relationship that these beings create together as you build your altar. Your altar can be the same each time, or you can use different arrangements and items depending on what is calling to you. Feel your body and listen to your soul as you choose your medicine items and bring together your altar. This is deeply sacred work that is setting the stage for your Earth-healing practice.

Once you have these basic materials for your altar, find a bag or basket to put them in. It's very useful to be able to take your medicine things with you when you go outside or go to various locations to make your ceremonies. When working with others, you can fashion altars together, blending your medicine items.

If you want to create a ritual at a time and place when you do not have your medicine bag or basket, you can use anything that you find in your environment. Ask your helping spirits to guide you to things that will help you build a healing ceremony. If you are outdoors, this is very easy to do. Feel in your body and ask to be led to any nature beings that want to be a part of your work. Always ask them before you pick them up to use in your ceremony. If you feel led to take something with you to add to your altar, ask the being if this is something that they want to do. Also, we do not own the things on our altars. Nature beings have their own path and will sometimes indicate that they want to be left in a location or sent with another person. While it can be hard to part with medicine things that are very important and meaningful, it is important to let them move on to where they belong and allow ourselves to open to new medicine. Always end any work with sacred things with gratitude for their help in your healing work.

EXERCISE: Listening to Your Sacred Stones

Purpose

This practice invites engaging your sacred stones, one at a time, slowly and with purpose as part of creating sacred space. Engaging body, senses and heart, this exercise deepens connection with our sacred stones while opening channels to dream with the Earth. To begin work with your own set of sacred stones, begin with the exercise Creating a Set of Sacred Stones, from Chapter Six.

During a shamanic ecotherapy workshop, as I put the processes of slowing down more fully into practice with the group, I developed this idea for meditating through our bodies and emotions with the sacred stones. This process deepened the connection for participants, and many finally said, "Now I get it." Slowing down is essential for the magic to emerge. In stillness, shifting time, we can begin to "feel the magic." After this simple exercise with your rocks, you may experience increased synchronicity, and a sense of "flow." Rocks are the guardians and wisdom of flow: of rivers, oceans, beaches, pressures of the Earth, rhythms of decomposition and formation from decay. When we slow our flow to connect with the time sense of rocks, we enter time from a different angle, allowing the web of life to appear to us.

Description

Find a comfortable place to sit or lie down. Plan to be uninterrupted for 90 minutes; this provides plenty of time to settle into your place, to welcome your stones into a sacred alignment and to complete and reflect on your experience. You can shorten the exercise if you need to; simply doing it is the most important thing. Sometimes, seeking perfection blocks our moments to connect, so do your best given your location and time constraints. I like to play soothing or meditative music while I listen to my stones. If it's warm, you can find a place where you will hear the music of the trees, birds, a river or creek, or the ocean. Create a ritual for yourself that covers each step in order, adjusting to the amount of time that you have and to your location.

Choose a method to keep time. I do so by counting my breaths, but you can find and use your own method. However you keep time when you meditate will work. Spend seven minutes with each stone, gazing, feeling it, speaking to it, listening, reading the images and textures. Ask it questions; imagine where it came from and why it's here with you now. Press it against your heart and love it; if it's hard to feel love for a rock, imagine that you love it. But rocks can be very relational, which is often very surprising to people as, in Western culture, we perceive them as quite inanimate. They are ancient and know the original dream of the spirit of Gaia. They will speak their wisdom and guide us when we listen.

When you are finished, feel in your body the vibration of each stone and let them speak to you to find a correlation with the elemental energies in the chart below.[91] If you feel a connection with a certain stone, but not a correlation between this stone and the elemental energies described on the chart, remain connected with that stone, but put it aside for now and seek another for your set of seven. Another way to more slowly let the stones open up their wisdom is to place them under your pillow, or near your bed, while you sleep, and ask for dreams from the stone to help you understand their energetic imprint and feel their relevance to your healing, as well as the healing of others that you might work with in ceremony.

Earth	Water	Fire	Air	Spirit	Crossing the Veil	Cosmos
Land Self	Sea Self	Fire Self	Talking Self	Higher Self	Non-ordinary States	Oneness Universe
Body Practicality	Feeling	Will	Intellect	Radiance	Synchronicity	Universe
Balance	Emotions	Sexuality	Mind	Integration	Intuition	Planetary Relationships
Bones	Relations	Creativity	Clarity	Synthesis	Soul	Star Systems
Stones	Fluids	Energy	Breath	Soul Guides	Shamanic States	Our Sun
	Subconscious	Passion	Ancestors			

Ritual Circles with Your Sacred Stones

As you continue developing your Earth Spirit Dreaming practice, creating and working with circles with your sacred stones, or any stones, integrates many of the essential ingredients of an Earth Spirit Dreaming experience into one activity. In the next chapter, we will move into visioning work with mandalas. For now, as you increase your comfort with creating sacred space for Earth Spirit Dreaming experiences, exploring ways to incorporate your sacred stones into your rituals will deepen your understanding of the stones. Allow the stones to guide you in relationship as you discover and create new forms of ritual in your own way. Doing this is an exercise in growing intuition and relationship with the stones. Trust yourself and feel into your body to find direction in working with your sacred stones.

In my personal spiritual work, and in the Earth Spirit Dreaming method, circle symbolism reflected in mandalas is a central feature of rituals, ceremonies and visioning work. The beauty of using sacred mandalas as an Earth Spirit Dreaming practice is that creating a mandala as ceremony contains every aspect of a visioning ritual. Mandalas are outer expressions of inner revelation and also create a map to discover flashes of insight and development. The next chapter leads from creating rituals quite naturally into working with mandalas, expressions of our self in relation to all of life and a representation of the cosmos.

15

Dreaming with Mandalas: Journeying with Sacred Circles

It is difficult to explain the power and potency of mandala work: it is felt and learned through experience. My own mandala meditations are sometimes minutes, sometimes hours, sometimes days. The longer you take to work with mandalas, the more the Orphic brilliance of the circle as a divine symbol will reveal itself to you.

Mandalas are my primary spiritual system for healing and leadership, and for bringing my spiritual mission to fruition on the planet. I nurture many mandalas of different sizes, and in varying locations, for different lengths of time as a regular practice. From this commitment to my practice, I now sense their vibrational power as portals into non-ordinary states.

The depth of self-realization available through working with mandalas provides exceptional topography for visioning. There are myriad systems and styles of mandala work available within many cultural frameworks, and mandalas work quite well as instruments for actualization without the need for complex knowledge and methods for using them. The beauty of this time on Earth is that human wisdom traditions can come together through technologies that allow us to share knowledge in unprecedented ways.

When working with mandalas, we can blend traditions of self-healing to further our spiritual development. So, if you already understand and work with mandalas from any tradition, you may bring this knowledge forth in your Earth Spirit Dreaming visioning process as long as you are true to the intention of the work: to bring our lives into alignment for the healing of the world.

EXERCISE: Visioning Collage Mandala

Purpose

This practice allows the release of the rational orientation of our minds through creative connection with sacred circles. Collage work invites us into embodied imaginal experience. The images in our magazine as we turn the pages, tuning in to our intuition to feel our way toward images that attract us, cutting, feeling the texture of paper, the smell of ink and glue: all of these sensations bring back emotions and memories of childhood, when we knew imaginal experience as a natural state of being. Collage takes us back to this simplicity, a "less is more" state of relaxed intuition. The many sense experiences opened through collage work segue beautifully into the mysteries of mandalas.

With our creativity awake and active, collage mandalas allow us to become submerged in symbols that speak directly from our souls. When making a visioning collage mandala, I ask my helping spirits to direct me. I imagine a beam of light coming through the top of my head and down through my hands. I open to receive images that will guide me beyond my own limitations to create a vision that is oriented toward healing. I trust my body and my imagination to listen to the voice of my spirit as I unearth the depths of my soul.

Description

Begin by gathering your materials for this exercise. Easy and simple materials are fine. If you have one magazine, use one magazine; use more if you have them. Any paper of any size will do. Often, if I can't find paper, I grab a piece from the printer or turn over a piece of paper that I pull from the recycling. For this exercise, the goal is not to create a collage to hang on your wall as art, but to listen to your inner self (though many of mine do hang on my wall as reminders from my higher, Earth-connected self). If nothing is on hand, a quick trip to an arts/craft store can offer affordable materials.

Children's sections are particularly great. If this becomes a practice that is meaningful and important to you, you can begin collecting more materials: paper of different sizes, glue that you like (I prefer glue sticks) and a dedicated place to do this form of spirit art. A kitchen table or the floor, or a place outside, are great places to start.

First, open ritual space and connect with Earth and Spirit using practices from earlier in the book so that you are visioning from a place of high vibration. Set a clear intention, as discussed in the introduction above. Allow an intention for your collage to emerge through your art while opening to a circular relationship among the images. I sometimes begin by drawing a circle on the paper as a guide, or by intentionally creating a circle with my images as a starting point. Collage mandalas sometimes include part of a circle, many circles, quadrants and many other variations.

There is no right way to create your collage mandala. As you work, and open to your symbolic knowing by moving your hands, enjoying textures, relishing the beauty of images, let feelings, impressions, images and ideas float up from your depths.

EXERCISE: Circling Mandala Meditation
Purpose

The word mandala means "circle" in Sanskrit, and all mandalas incorporate circles in some way. Relating to these symbolic circles helps us understand ourselves in relation to all of life; they are personal and spiritual developmental tools in many cultural traditions. Thus, working with them helps us to restore and maintain balance and health. The quadrants of the mandalas represent the integration of differentiation and wholeness. Mandalas help us sense the whole in the parts, and the parts in relation to the whole in the world, as well as within ourselves.

This simple practice utilizes the quadrants of the mandala to manifest visions in relationship to the directions, and in various aspects of the quadrants in relation to one another. As you move through this practice of building and circling the mandala, record any thoughts, images or physical sensations that come to you. Draw an image of the mandala in the circle and note where you were in the mandala when each realization or experience occurred. This will help you read the meanings of your visioning when reflecting on your meditation.

Description

Your supplies for the mandala can be simple. Using your sacred stones and your medicine things is a good place to start. You can do this exercise using just your stones and medicine objects or incorporate them as a center or part of a larger mandala with other stones, leaves, sticks, candles, sacred herbs, pine cones and any other art or sacred objects that bring you positive feelings. If you are outdoors without your altar things, nature beings as simple as leaves and grass, and small rocks and sticks, work well for creating a mandala.

Begin your mandala visioning ceremony with the steps of a sacred ritual. Your mandala does not need to be done in any particular way. Sometimes a "nothing special" approach can help liberate us to be free with our intuition as the mandala emerges. Let your mandala come into form in reverence, playfulness and joy. Allow yourself to be as a child, if you can, bearing in mind that in any ceremony, all states and feelings are welcome. Often, we go to mandala work with feelings of sadness, grief, fear or any other possible range of feelings. Let yourself be as you are. There is no right or wrong way to make or be with your mandala, as long as you have followed the ritual protocols to set a healing intention for the experience. Start with a circle and follow your feelings from there. Making a simple circle is the mandala; everything else is an expression of your spirit and psyche in relationship to the Earth and cosmos at any given time.

If you have time and are planning ahead, ask for dreams, places and symbols that stand out to you during the days or weeks ahead of your mandala ritual. Watch for synchronicities to guide you to the right time, place and materials to use for your mandala. Trust your feelings, even if they seem quite out of the ordinary; this is the mandala gateway to magic already beginning to open. Once we intend to create a ritual in our hearts, the web for the ritual begins in that moment.

To create your mandala, begin with a circle and place something in the center to represent spirit, as well as the center of yourself in relation to spirit. I also include the elements of water and air, usually with a container holding water, and with smudging of some kind. Air is also in the wind, so if you are outside, this is your air element. I often light candles, to bring in the element of fire. And, since I'm using things from nature, I am honoring Earth. You can intentionally align the four points of the circle with the directions (north, south, east, west), or not. Sometimes waiting to see where the alignments end up without consciously placing them proves to be an interesting part of the visioning process.

Depending on the size of your mandala, you can meditate sitting inside or outside the circle. I enjoy building a mandala large enough to allow me to sit in each quadrant (you can do this inside or outside, sitting on the ground or in a chair that you move around the mandala). If you don't have this kind of space, meditate around the quadrants on the outside of the circle. You can choose an amount of time to meditate in each quadrant, keeping time with a timekeeper or by counting your breaths. I count a certain number of breaths in each quadrant, which works as a helpful mindfulness and centering method as I move through the ritual. Also feel free to follow your intuition to decide when to move to the next quadrant.

Circling a mandala is a profound practice for connecting with this ancient divine oracle. A powerful healing symbol of personal growth, mandalas are a portal to feeling ourselves within the matrix of multiple intelligences. Often, in the moment with the mandala it may seem that nothing is happening. The messages may come later. Sometimes, feelings and messages can feel like a crashing wave flowing through you. However the mandala opens to you, invite the feelings to emerge slowly. It is okay to consciously adjust the "flow" of the energy of the mandala. Ask for more or less energy from the mandala as you want or need to during your meditation. Try to let your mind go during your time with the mandala. If your mind stays busy, honor that and just say "thinking" softly to yourself, then return to watching and feeling the beauty of the mandala.

If you do have time, commit a full day or more to working with a particular mandala. Or commit to create a new mandala to work with every day. You can go back again and again to the same mandalas. I have a few in different outdoor locations that I work with alone and with others over days, months and years.

EXERCISE: Inviting Spirit Symbols with Mandalas

Purpose

Along with stone circles, we can also draw mandalas to open to symbolic and wisdom knowing. Drawing mandalas is a sacred art form. The simple act of drawing mandala images creates shifts in the physical, emotional and spiritual body. While mandalas can be complex and entrancing works of art, simple drawings with a focus on process rather than product is the goal in this exercise. I invite you to use this practice of drawing mandalas to open to your own guidance and intuition, and to receive guidance from Earth and Spirit. If you are drawing your mandala outside, this sacred art practice will help to open your natural sensitivities to the elemental nature energies.

Description

First, collect your materials: large paper or poster boards, markers, colored pencils, crayons. Create your ritual using the steps described in Chapter Fourteen.

To start your mandala, draw a circle of any size. Let an image, shape, a word or an idea come to you. Notice feelings in your body or memories and begin to represent these in any way that you want to on your mandala. Pictures, colors, blobs, scratches, scribbles are all welcome. This is not art as we tend to understand it, but rather as a psycho-spiritual process. You can put your image in the mandala in any way, location, size or method that occurs to you. Trust the unfolding process, let your hands move and try not to think!

As an addition to a circling mandala meditation, you can draw a mandala as described in this exercise and then cut or tear it into pieces in any way that inspires you. Use these pieces as part of creating a meditation mandala or add them to a mandala that you're already working with. You can also create a karmic eddies mandala, as described in Chapter Twelve, then cut or tear that mandala into pieces and use those cut-outs with the circling mandala meditation.

Using your drawn mandalas that represent specific aspects of your life with a larger and longer circling mandala meditation is particularly useful for visioning for personal healing and guidance from the spirit helpers with specific issues that may be pressing on, blocking or causing you pain. Healing and clearing in our own lives is always healing the world; the microcosm of our own work to grow and change mirrors the issues requiring attention on a global level.

If you have time, commit a full day or more to working with a particular mandala. Or commit to creating a new mandala to work with every day. Setting up repetitious and consistent methods to work with your mandalas will help you move into the power and symbolic magic of these sacred circles. You can construct them inside or out and go back again and again to the same mandalas over long periods of time. I have a few in different outdoor locations that I work with alone and with others over days, months and years.

Over time your relationship with the energies and helping spirits called into and through each circle will deepen. It was my two-year relationship with the medicine wheel behind my house that led me to my call as a healer and it was there that I crossed over into shamanic reality for the first time. I did not expect or consciously seek these particular experiences. My intentions to seek guidance through the power of sacred mandala ceremonies called the spirits and energies that led me more fully into my spiritual mission. Ask the Earth and spirit helpers to guide you and wait for the gateways to open, remembering that the magic is often just next to and within the most ordinary moments.

EXERCISE: Working with Visioning Rocks

Purpose

The Earth Spirit Dreaming approach continually returns to the voices and energies of rocks to reveal a healing dream for Gaia. This focus on rocks represents their significance to my own path of awakening. I also know from experience that they hold ancient body memories of the planet. Their knowing and relationship to time is long, deep and broad, reaching to the heart and consciousness of the Earth. Learning to speak with the rocks, the "stone people," is a life-changing skill and a path to true Earth magic.

Description

If you already work with your own set of sacred stones, as described in the exercise Creating a Set of Sacred Stones from Chapter Six, you can start visioning with them as you begin to know them deeply by creating the sacred bond between you. Knowing the stone people comes with intentionally cultivating a relationship with these beings, as you would a friend or cherished family member. Stones are truly wisdom ancestors as they were here long before us and will remain long after we are gone.

To vision with stones, you can work with a rock nearby, new or already known to you. You can also invite a specific vision stone to come to you, by inviting a stone already in your circle to be your vision rock or by asking spirit helpers to lead you to a place and time to meet a vision rock. As you choose a visioning rock, you are opening a connection with the rock by bringing reverence to the process.

Follow the steps to create a ritual and set the intention for visioning with the rock. When you reach the part of your ritual to begin visioning, open a communication by asking the rock if they want to engage in a visioning process with you and thank them for making this connection. Feel the rock with all of your senses. Take your time caressing the rock and holding it with love. Meditate with the rock on your altar, or in a mandala that you've made, while gazing at the surface textures and crevices. Allow your vision to go soft and see what images and impressions might emerge.

To enhance your visioning in a circling mandala meditation, focus on your visioning rock in the center of a meditation mandala. Images will begin to emerge in the rock, along with memories from your life, past and present, and sometimes even past lives. Visioning rocks are a window to your own soul and the soul of the world, so you may find that deep, sometimes overwhelming feelings emerge. Also, pay attention to sensations in your body and write them down, along with any animals that emerge as pictures in the visioning stone.

Any thoughts or feelings that we have while immersed in sacred communication with visioning rocks cannot be separated into only our own or only the rock's reality. The process of visioning with rocks is deeply co-creative and primal. Visions with rocks emerge in the context of the geological time memories that are inherent in "rock-ness." The first pictures are often projections of our personal hopes and fears. During this time, we may get answers or comfort regarding current situations in our lives. The first period of visioning is a bit like a Rorschach test in that things that are going on in our interiors can show up in pictures on the rocks. This is one way that rocks acknowledge you just as you are acknowledging them.

Now you have started cultivating a relationship with a vision rock, and can bring it into your circling mandala meditation. Thus, your sacred mandalas become stacked with levels of meaning and communication including portals to Earth body memories and spirit worlds, ancestors and light beings. The spiritual net that you create through committed work with healing mandalas and vision stones reaches all around you, across time and space, with broad and deep roots into the web of life that is on, within and surrounding the Earth.

Animals will often appear as images in your vision stone, as well as faces, places and things. While I'm working with my primary outdoor spirit mandala, sometimes deer come from the woods and walk around my circle or across certain quadrants; owls land behind me, hawks call above me; bees, spiders and bugs of all kinds will make their way across my circle. Sometimes there may even be a snake. As soon as you complete a visioning cycle, write down all of these images and encounters. You can later journey to find out more or ask for dreams to come to help you understand your visions with the rocks.

Keep track of these images, sensations, and any feeling or memories, as they are all part of the complex visioning process. You can also later evaluate the location and direction of your images and feelings, and often find guidance for healing and unfolding life direction depending on where you were in relation to the directions when certain images arose. The longer you watch a visioning stone, the more fluid and magical the pictures will become. Often, it can feel that layers are peeling away to take you further and further across time, either backward or forward. Miracles can happen as you deepen this practice.

Reading the Oracle

Interpreting symbolic wisdom from our visioning work is a tricky business. Our rapid information culture, and addiction to linear and reductive ways of knowing, can short-circuit the process. Complex spirit information can be mystifyingly symbolic and non-linear and take long periods of time to unfold as meaning and purpose in our human terms. This is because the information that we receive from contact with the cosmos comes through our wisdom selves.

This information does not fit well within the limits and confines of our brain-minds. To be effective dreamers for the Earth we must relate to symbolic knowing with our larger heart-minds. Much of the knowing that comes to us as visions and dreams may never make sense to us, except in small, sometimes very strange-seeming flashes. Rather, we engage these visions with our heart-minds, embracing them with gratitude and love and accepting that we can only find a path back to the Divine with much help. We come to feel deep in our bones that we truly are never alone. And while visioning with the Earth and spirit realms helps us feel more at home and loved than ever before, the trade-off is that we again and again release control of our separate ego selves to allow communion with the embedded nature of our true selves.

Through dreaming and visioning we develop a broader capacity for paradox. Allow yourself to be with the discomfort of not knowing in your head what the symbols that come to you in visions mean. Let your heart feel the support and love, and deep wisdom, shared with you from the spirit and nature intelligences. This form of visioning is a relational process that unfolds over time and with practice.

If you are really eager to understand, and your desire to know with your head is creating a block for you, you can begin learning the common meanings of symbols as a step toward understanding. Reading mythology, dream symbolism, animal meanings, spirit and animal cards may help you begin to feel oriented in a sometimes confusing and overwhelming sea of newness. Eventually, the best approach is to meet each symbol or being on their own terms. An excellent way to proceed is to ask the symbol, picture, whatever emerges, to express its meaning and purpose to you. Ask for a dream, spend some time taking shamanic journeys to this image, symbol, feelings or being. Draw it, doodle it, picture it and send it light from your heart. In all things, send gratitude for this supportive vision and to the beings and guides that have sent it to you. Love, light and gratitude are the most effective means for deepening relationships to and understanding of messages and messengers.

Also, look for similar images popping up in your life. I had an oracular dream with an image that came up in my life repeatedly at pivotal decision points as I was choosing to follow a spirit path that my personal self resisted quite fiercely at times. This was an image of two faces together, and it popped up in my life in many different settings. The when and where of these appearances helped me understand where to go and when, on an otherwise opaque path to a new way of being in my life. Eventually, this one image unfolded into my spirit guides giving me a spirit name in the shamanic realm. River Light eventually emerged from these two faces.

I first had the dream the night before attending a healing dream workshop led by my friend and colleague, Christopher Reynolds. He suggested that we invite dreams before arriving. I had a long dream where I was leading people into the Earth. Some sort of symbolic alphabet greeted us as we moved in, in long lines. I realized that we had lost the ability to understand this language, and that it was my job to help us return to this understanding. I was then standing on an earthen mound covered with grass and I had a two-sided face. This felt so important at the time, but I had no idea why. This image led me continually as I made many difficult and challenging choices to move more fully into my spiritual mission over the next few years; and it continues to guide me.

Letting new dreams and stories come forth from our connection with the web of life begins by learning to work with symbols and visions through ceremony and ritual. Extrasensory experiences to seek and create visions of healing begin with opening the gateway of the imagination, through revelatory art forms that teach us a language of symbols and imaginal reality. In the next chapter, we see how the imaginal and symbolic realms are reached through creating conditions for extrasensory perception through guided meditations and shamanic journeying. With careful preparation from previous practices, we learn to spiral further into altered states step by step. We then can communicate with nature "spirits," or the energetic imprint of nature beings, and relate directly to our personal spirit helpers and the higher planetary guides orchestrating the shifts on consciousness happening now all across the planet.

16

Dancing with the Ancestors: Cultivating Shamanic Experience

Discovering magic happens through fostering gateways to mysterious encounters and feelings that intertwine with and exist beyond causal-linear reality. We are not taught to relate to and hold the deep magic and mystery that are hallmarks of fully actualized existence. Magical encounters and leaps of creativity into numinous knowing do not fit into accepted reductionist and instrumental concepts of what is "real" in the world. Our ancestors knew the ways of conscious dreaming: bringing forth each new day in communion with the ancestors and spirits of the Earth; speaking of visions and sightings across the veil; making dreaming the world into being a central and honored place in the circle of community.

We are all equipped with the tools needed to foster shamanic experience. The most basic things that any child likes to do are the means. Joy, play, dance, song, wonder, full feeling, complete presence: these are the ways to open the gates, and they are readily available to all of us. Music, art and dance are natural creative resources to express feelings and connection with the magic and mystery of the Divine. These basic human functions are a daily need and a wellspring of joy and relationship with each other and the cosmos in all her expressions. I play my clay flute, or other music, to start any ritual. A song that came to me in my giant meditation mandala in the woods behind my house calls the ancestors, and the spirits of the Earth and sky to me, and to those who join me in the circle of Earth-honoring reverence. In ritual circles — particularly the ones that I create and nurture regularly — I feel vortices of open communication with the memories of the Earth and the voices and visions of the helping spirits. Engaged through meditation with nature, listening and speaking with Earth and all beings of life, I open a doorway of divine love in my heart to raise the vibrations for pathways of communication across the veils of space and time. I engage in my daily Earth healing practices, hands on the Earth outside, or holding her in my arms in the eye of my imagination. As I shift perceptions, move deliberately through ritual into trance, eventually the ancient Earth wildness, ancestors dancing, body memories of the Earth, impressions of spirit helpers, entrée into quantum intelligence, reveal themselves to me.

I play my flute and sing a song as a gift to the helping spirits and the nature energies all around, giving the gifts of gratitude and joy for this life that is supported and possible in every moment because of the Earth and Divine Spirit that animates my soul. Listening to my heartbeat, I drum with the slow thrumming of the Earth's breathing, the moving of water under and over her skin; the waves, the skies opening with wind and rain. Listening to the Earth, and the patterns of my own breathing as it works in rhythm with my heart, I enter the pulse of life.

In my journey, the rhythms and rituals of the sacred creativity of ceremony open my senses to the ancestors, the elemental nature energies and the spirit helpers. Drumming, singing and making art open my mind and I wander with intention across veils, into other realms. As in many journeys, I hear faraway drumming. Slowly, over time, I move through the woods in the middle world closer to this sound. I begin to see fire flickering through the darkness, beams breaking through the brush and trees where the ancestors inhabit the forest.

Each time I go there, I move a bit closer. Eventually, I am peering through trees. One time I take a step into the circle as my true self. They know me; they have been waiting for me. One day, I step into the circle to dance. No hesitation, no wondering, no decision, no mind. I am just one with my ancestors; my feet bless the Earth in a circle of my people. Joy, celebration, admiration, oneness of mind and purpose and consciousness with my family.

Why Do We Say Shaman?

These magical moments that happen as we re-indigenize Western minds are unexplainable to Western people because the nomenclature and necessary categories of understanding needed for these kinds of knowing are profoundly atrophied. Access to magic is a gift in our DNA from our ancestors, and they cheer us on as we find new ways to dance with time out of time. Yet, there is a struggle, and a bit of staggering through, as we find our way to a shared language for the emergence of the shamanic experience in Western culture in this time and place. Words that don't quite fit, or are overused, are the best we can do sometimes.

I have struggled in the past with using the word "shamanic" to define the experiences that are now regular occurrences for me after years of meditating and making art and music in nature. I did not consciously seek out shamanic experience and was very resistant to the idea when I realized that my experiences fit best into what this word generally means — and what it now fails to mean because of being so overused outside of indigenized experience community. I did not train with a shaman or seek to become a shaman. I do not consider myself a shaman or think that this book will train others to become shamans. Rather, I think that what we think of as altered states and "shamanic experience" are everyday states in many indigenous cultures that we need to relearn.

Despite my discomfort with the term "shaman," or "shamanic," after much reading and exploring, I think this is the best word to fit with the kinds of perceptions I seek to describe. The word is at this point very watered down, overused and distorted in Western culture, as is our relationship to magical, mysterious and complex spiritual experiences. Our distorted and lost relationship with the word reflects our discordant and lost relationship with the aspects of human life that the word represents. Yet, shamanism is the first religion of the human species, and is accessible to all people through natural senses that everyone can develop over time.

Shamanism was the religion of my indigenous, northern European ancestors. All of our ancestral roots lead back to shamanic culture at some point in the past. Within our traditional religions are vestiges of shamanism, some containing more shamanic elements than others. Our natural wonder and awe of nature is the basis of shamanic experience.

Due to the immense and painful appropriation and annihilation of indigenous cultures by Western people, as well as the other reservations previously discussed, I have tried finding and using many other words to describe these kinds of experiences. After much reflection, for lack of a better term, to help reclaim and contextualize the word and because the perceptions and practices that I'm discussing here fit the traditional elements of shamanism, I use this word now, with some reservations but also with hope and confidence that we can reorient and reframe the term through authentic practice. The perceptions and practices that make this word fit are:

- mindful, embodied Earth-connected awareness
- understanding and sensing life as a web of energetic/light connections
- working with vibrational and energy reality for healing and change
- using trance states to connect with spirit helpers and guides
- traveling in other "worlds" to seek guidance and healing
- and seeking ways of symbolic knowing, or "dream" knowing.

I now believe that shamanic experience is in our DNA and speaks to something deep and primal within us. Shamanism awakens Earth and spiritual intelligence, which are desperately needed to face the profound challenges we face on the planet at this time.

A note on "other realms": I believe firmly, as I've stated before in this book, that we cannot understand the profound complexity of life or the cosmos/universe, and much of what we encounter in spirit realms, but we can relate to what exists in these realms. In my own guiding understanding of my extrasensory experience, I see the presentation of imagery, locations and beings to be a choice in the moment between myself and the being, or beings, I am connecting with for a specific purpose, intention or communication. Without a doubt, there are common experiences, types of locations and symbols/archetypes that emerge again and again, across cultures and throughout human history, for those of us who travel in these realms. For me, I see the "stories" and locations of my encounters as a container that allows my human mind and understanding to experience these profound beings, messages and information through the lens of the perceptual instrument of my human form. In other words, I don't know that these locations exist "out there"; in fact I don't personally think that they do — rather I think that they are created in a shared space as I meet with spirit beings. This view reminds me that we are share-dreaming even our everyday Earth reality into existence, just as I share-dream a common space with spirit helpers and guides.

Trance States for Extrasensory Perception

This chapter introduces readers to practices that use extrasensory experiences to seek and create visions of healing for themselves and the world. The shamanic states that these exercises support can be considered "light" trance states, in that you are still mostly aware of yourself and what is going on around you while you are exploring reality through extrasensory perception. Deeper trance states can be reached through similar methods practiced over longer periods of time with increased intensity. Deep trance states should be reserved for places with appropriate community, training and ritual support for the one doing the deep trance visioning.

For the purposes of Earth Spirit Dreaming, light trance states, from which we can emerge relatively easily, are the goal. Still, since your perceptions are altered after these practices, it is important to very intentionally return to your body and "everyday" reality through grounding methods. Earth grounding helps us feel centered and balanced as we begin to "walk between worlds," which is, along with many other reasons, why it is an essential step of Earth Spirit Dreaming. When beginning to work with trance states, you may sometimes feel that you are in a dream, or that things don't feel real, even when you are not doing the visioning rituals or practices. When this happens, do things that stimulate your "normal" senses: eat fragrant foods, dip your hands in water, walk barefoot on the ground, lightly pat or tap your body and the top of your head, wiggle your toes, tap your feet on the ground. Your body is your friend when holding and learning to manage trance states. Consciously stay in your body as much as you can.

In shamanic practice, the imaginal and symbolic realms are reached through creating conditions for extrasensory perception. The Earth and Spirit methods from previous chapters help you reach the threshold of trance states, and practices from the last chapter bring you to gateways of numinous experience. In this chapter, we will use practices to bring you past the edge of magic into the fully magical, quantum, non-local and non-linear shamanic realms.

Once we set the stage — ground to earth, create the correct vibrational reality, set our intentions — we begin the primary work of moving into shamanic reality with drumming. The drum is the main medicine of the shaman. While we are exploring shamanic experience, we learn to work with drumming, dancing and singing to reach trance states. We approach these tools and methods with great care and reverence as we remember how to be magical beings once more.

The primary methods for reaching trance states, not including plant medicines, focus on basic human creative expressions: drumming, dancing, singing, making music in other ways, creative expression through art, through mask making, body paint, and many more. For our purposes, in this chapter we will focus on drumming, dancing and singing, building upon the sacred creativity of the rituals we use to support this work. Dancing, singing and making rhythm are basic for all humans as celebratory and expressive acts.

We raise vibrations through music and dance, and fundamentally enhance and alter our feelings in many ways. In *Healing Across Cultures & the Good Life*, the authors describe the type of drumming and movement that induce trance states as:

> *Repetitive, long-lasting, constant beats with concerted focus, and chanting repeatedly with constancy ... Many anthropologists have seen how music that urges dancing profoundly alters the structure*

of one's consciousness, changing how one experiences both space and time ...

The many forms of constant, rhythmic percussion, such as with drums, rattles, or gongs, produce the phenomenon of entrainment. Entrainment occurs when the asynchronous patterns of the brain waves come into harmonic resonance.[92]

EXERCISE: Creating Your Sacred Space in Shamanic Reality
Purpose

This simple visualization guides us to create a safe and very personal place in the imaginal realms. This is a place to return to again and again, and to discover and rest in your true self. Experience of our true selves recharges us for our work for the Earth and helps to guide us back to ourselves and our spiritual mission.[93]

This guided visualization came to me in the mid-nineties, as I struggled through deep trauma work. I created a visualization, putting together a variety of guided meditations that I was working with at the time. Later, I learned that I had found my way to what some shamanic traditions call "the lower world." It is a realm of consciousness close to the Earth's center where fecund and primal energies reside. This guided visualization takes us back to our source, our beginnings and what has come before for us in past lives and earlier in this life. Eventually, entering the lower world in shamanic journeys will bring us to a place from which to engage our shadow and reclaim lost aspects of ourselves (also called soul retrieval). It is a place for foundational and intense healing work.

For now, the goal is to find a safe and grounding place at the entry to this realm of shared consciousness using your imagination. We will only go to the opening place of the lower world and find a central and safe place from which to rest and restore our energies. Note: do not move past the initial entry place in this realm without the guidance of a trained and trusted shamanic guide. Self-guided soul retrieval work is only to be done after much personal growth, and shamanic training and experience. Until then, work with a well-trained and supportive guide.

Description

Find a safe and comfortable place to rest, either sitting or lying down. Try to limit interruptions for 30 minutes. Create your sacred place using the ritual methods and order from Chapter Fourteen. As you move into the visualization, remember that your imagination is your gateway to the imaginal realms. You are co-creating this sacred space for yourself, so feel free to trust the images and impressions that feel right to you. To follow the visualization, you can read it beforehand or make a recording of it.

Imagine that you're walking down a hallway. Feel your feet on the floor. Imagine your shoes lightly stepping on the floor, making a soft noise. You walk with purpose down this hallway. Soon, the walls begin to turn red. As this happens, imagine everything that you associate with the color red. Visualize these things you imagine and feel the sensations of them. Strawberries, soft and juicy, sweet and fragrant. Pomegranates, with all the seeds filling up the fruit like stars. Imagine a cool, red mist infusing your body.

You begin to feel that you're floating on this red mist. As you step along a few inches from the ground this mist begins to turn orange. You smell the tart sweetness of oranges all around you as you continue to step softly through this tunnel. The orange, fragrant mist surrounds you and supports you. You feel warm and safe in this orange glow that carries you along as you step softly forward.

You begin to smell lemons as the mist turns to yellow. The yellow mist clears to allow bright, warm sunlight to fall across your face and shoulders. You look down to see that you're barefoot now, and walking on soft, warm sand. You continue to step across this sand as the walls of the tunnel expand away from you and disappear. As you gaze at the sunlight falling all around you, you see trees just ahead with the light filtering softly through the leaves.

The light splits into beams that fall toward the ground in long shafts. You hear the wind moving in the leaves and continue to walk until you enter the coolness of the forest. Smell the loamy earth of the forest floor around you and feel the softness of leaves and soft dirt under your feet.

You look down to see a path as you continue to move forward, step by soft step, feeling your feet roll onto the forest floor as you walk. As you continue down this path, you begin to see a clear, small lake ahead of you. The blue is almost aqua by the shore, becoming darker where the water deepens. There are rounded, hand-sized rocks all along the shore in shades of white and soft gray and the lightest coral. The rocks feel cool and smooth beneath your feet as you continue to walk, allowing your feet to enter the water. You feel relaxed in this water, as if it is the safest place on Earth, a womb, a vessel. You know that you will be able to swim and breathe easily in this water as the memories of being in the womb come back to you. You walk further into the water until you are swimming. You swim down into the dark deep blue of the water, feeling the cool water holding you weightless and buoyant.

As you swim, you see a beautiful indigo light in front of you: an orb that grows as you move through it. As you swim closer to this bright, vibrant, undulating circle of light, you notice that it's a gateway. You see a violet center in the orb, with a pinprick of light shooting through it. You continue to swim and the light grows until you see dry land on the other side. You realize that this is a portal between two realms. You feel beckoned to step through this shimmering wall of light as you see soft images begin to appear to you on the other side. You swim toward the portal and step onto the floor of the lake. You reach one leg through the gate, then move your whole body onto the other side into a dry, safe world. You meet a being just as you enter the realm. You ask, "May I enter?" The being nods, inviting you to pass with a turn of the body. Before you, you see a circle of land, somewhat like an island, with pathways leading in different directions toward unseen places. You know that your work today is to find a comfortable place here, leaving the pathways for another visit.

Picture the place where you are. It is natural and inviting, the landscape that you love best. Imagine the ground, the sky, the plants, trees and animals. You feel safety and love all around you as you imagine this place, which is the best place you can be. Your place. As you see this land come into form around you, you feel drawn toward a specific place on the island. Your heart begins to light up and pulse as you look around, and you begin to see a light calling to you.

You walk toward the light. As you come closer, you see a special place just for you begin to take shape. Notice what this place looks like, how it feels for you, what surrounds it. Is there an entrance to your special place? A path, a walkway, a door to enter? Let it emerge in your imagination as just the right place for you. Spend some time exploring your special place. Feel how deeply safe, relaxed and energized you feel in this place. Take time to experience all the details of your special place.

Once you feel comfortable, notice that there is something in your special place that offers you guidance. You can see, feel, touch or hear something to take back with you that comes easily to you through this unique feature of your special place. Let a gift come toward you that you will carry back or remember when you return to your everyday reality. Sit quietly in your place, relax, tell your place how grateful you are to be here and say thank you for the special gift. When you are ready, retrace your steps back to the indigo gateway that leads to the pond that you swam through earlier. Say thank you to the guide at the door. Then step through the violet light portal back into the cool water of the pond.

You easily swim to the surface, following the light of the sun. You come out of the water and find that you are on the shore, completely dry, just as the entrance to the path through the woods becomes visible. You walk back through the woods onto the sandy, warm, yellow expanse and see a door surrounded by yellow mist leading into a hallway. You step into the hallway, into orange mist that turns to a darker orange and then slowly into red. You feel yourself begin to breathe back into your body. You feel your feet where they press on the floor and you wiggle your toes, arriving fully and completely into the room where you started your journey. Now that you are back, you feel the safety and energy of your special place with you, and you know that you can go back there any time you want to.

EXERCISE: Visioning with Nature Beings — Becoming Fully Human
Purpose

As we move into re-indigenized ways of knowing, we can learn to speak and listen to nature "spirits." In Western culture, there is the "real" world and the spirit world. As we re-indigenize our bodies and minds these false separations begin to fall away, often engendering radical and shocking sensations and perceptions when relating to beings in nature. These beings always have stories, histories, families, memories, each in their own way. When we vision with these beings, we listen to their stories and their dreams, and release ourselves into co-mingling our boundaries. We become tree singers and river walkers. Feeling the motion of life through these beings' senses, our fingers become soft leaves blowing in the wind; we begin to sense the knowing of 500 years of old trees and millennia of mountains; a new bird is the greatest joy; the nature of death is a true opening. Visioning with nature beings, we move through the sky like the wind, hearing the names of the breezes floating above us like the birds. In this work, we become for a time the spirit of the nature beings and see through their eyes.

Description

When we are first starting to speak to nature beings, it can feel awkward and even ridiculous in the framework of Western "reason." I remind myself in these moments that while it may feel crazy to speak to beings in nature, the actual insanity we face derives from having forgotten how to speak with nature relatives and ancestors in the first place.

The most basic way to dream with beings in nature, and to connect with the elemental nature energies, is practice. In a similar way to acknowledging another person when we pass, we begin to acknowledge the being-ness of all of nature as we move through life. Just as we develop empathy with people over time, and come to understand their individuality as well as our commonalities, we can learn to relate with nature as we speak and communicate with nature beings every day.

Over time, we foster deep relationships with nature in general, and with individual nature beings. The river near my house is a dear friend and guide. She shows me the way in my life; she moves me softly or sometimes roughly toward my spirit mission. I ask her to speak and I listen. All that is good in my life in recent years has been guided and supported in some way by her.

Forming relationships with nature beings transforms into visioning with nature beings through time commitment. Just as we come to share a vision of life with people who are close to us and important in our lives, this process happens by getting to know individual nature beings, as well as the *nature* of these beings. So, I know particular rivers and creeks, and I know RIVER the element. River is an important friend and teacher for me, in this realm and in the shamanic realms. The more I focus my energy and time on fostering this relationship, the deeper my visioning for the world becomes through the prism of the river.

I have other nature and animal guides that invite me to connect with them and come to me to share their wisdom. Part of shamanic experience is to practice merging our consciousness with nature and animal beings, always with permission, care and gratitude. Eventually, the "practicing," the imagining, grows into the experience. It is important to ask for help, and let the nature spirits and animals teach us how to do this.

We are not meant to create stories only as ourselves. We alone as individuals, or as humans separated from the web of life, do not have the strength and courage needed to see the world as we have co-created it and to move into something new. On our own, we literally do not have the physical, emotional and psycho-spiritual capacity to do what is required to heal the world. We need the senses and magnitude of the entire Earth community to help us become fully human again, and in becoming fully human we play our part in returning to a balanced state of living with the planet.

EXERCISE: Creating Rituals for Trance States
Purpose

The Earth Spirit Dreaming approach is meant to teach readers to create a myriad of rituals to fulfill a variety of intentions and connect with many locations and combinations of people. Rituals are essential for healing and creative dreaming: for envisioning blueprints for transforming our stories. Rituals create the conditions for us to come into our full senses and draw in and from the power of our communities. Rituals also provide cues to our bodies, hearts and minds to move into receptive states for spiritual work.

We often want things quickly in Western culture. This can lead to an "anything goes" approach to journeying. We need to ground our spiritual work in sacred and carefully developed rituals to shift into new stories. Otherwise, we risk just creating more of the same problems and challenges that we are living with now. Awareness of our states, and clarity of our minds and hearts, allow us to move through shamanic reality with clear intention and results. We achieve this by grounding into our bodies and the Earth, asking for support and connection with Earth beings, nature spirits, ancestors, spirit helpers and the Creator of the Universe. To change our lives and our world, we need all of our many, powerful capacities. These can only evolve through consistent work with ceremony and ritual.

Description

The most important part of all shamanic work is to develop comfort and facility with rituals and ceremony. Going through them again and again is needed to bring forth your own heart wisdom and body intelligence. Well-intentioned sacred rituals, with clear intentions and methods, are the means to travel and dream in shamanic realms safely and responsibly.

The rituals built from previous chapters create the ground for shamanic experience. For those of you who are already comfortable and experienced with rituals, you can blend them with your own practice to move through the Earth Spirit Dreaming steps. Creating a sacred space, grounding and connecting with Earth and clearing the vibrational space are skills that everyone can develop. This book offers many options for creating and nurturing sacred space. Eventually, these suggestions will meld into rituals that work best for you in your own life and work.

To reach shamanic states in the Earth Spirit Dreaming method, create a ritual using the steps in order: at least one from each section. More time and more preparation with grounding and vibrational work will bring more profound "traveling" and connection in shamanic reality. And, as emphasized throughout this book, commitment to regular practice builds our capacity for shamanic experience over time.

When we reach these states, it's important to be as Earth-grounded and as vibrationally clear as possible, so always prepare as much as you can. We can only re-vision our world by healing and shifting the mindset that's created the current challenges that we face as a species. The first two steps, Earth and Spirit, assure us that our dreaming comes from a place of clarity and connection with the healing spirit and other beings that are helping shift our consciousness.

EXERCISE: Shamanic Journeying
Purpose

We journey to connect with benevolent, supportive energies of many kinds: spirit helpers, ancestors, nature spirits, divine cosmic light, the spirits of houses, places, endeavors, ideas...the list is almost endless. Everything in "normal" reality has an aspect or an imprint that we can relate with in the spirit realms, and there are many beings that are not from this reality. Journeying is a life-changing endeavor.

The more it is done, the more profound and magical it becomes, forever changing the way that we understand life. Eventually, the world all around begins to morph. Experience becomes infused with magical impressions and portals to new ways of knowing that are impossible to imagine from a mind deeply seated in and seeded from rational reality.

When beginning, focus on connecting with your spirit helpers. It is the spirit helpers that make journeying safe and useful. Journeying without the guidance of spirit helpers is like wandering through the world without a map, risking our lives with strangers. Every time you journey ask for a spirit helper to accompany you — not just any guide, a spirit helping guide.

A note of caution: While some shamanic practitioners journey to address issues with dark, lost or destructive energies, this is not the focus of the work in this book and should not be undertaken without very serious training in the protocols to do this kind of work. These are advanced skills that take many, many years to develop. Following the steps in this book is one way to ensure that you are working with benevolent energies for healing, and not inadvertently encountering other kinds of things that exist in shamanic reality.

This is another reason that creating sacred space and setting clear intentions is essential, especially for beginning and intermediate shamanic work. As a measure of how rare it is to reach the level of advanced shamanic training and experience to do healing work with dark energies, I should tell you that I have only met one person in my life who has this level of training and knowledge, after *decades* of training and experience. In general, Western people are all very young in terms of shamanic work, and it is *crucial* to engage with great humility.

Description

When journeying, always start with creating sacred space, grounding, clearing and setting a clear intention (as described earlier in this book). Ask for guidance from light beings that want to help you and ask for protection as you travel. When journeying, prepare, prepare, prepare! For me, the journeys are often not that long, but if I want clarity, I know that preparation is key. As this book describes in detail, grounding to the Earth and Spirit/vibrational realms creates a centered place from which to journey and vision. If we journey from a disconnected, jumbled mind that is grounded in the dominant global consciousness, this is what we will bring back and recreate again and again.

Meditate, dance, sing, drum: do everything you can to raise your vibrations and shift into symbolic knowing/embodied mind. Leave your worries at the door. They will be there to pick up when you're done with your journey. Below are some steps to shamanic journeying. Though there are many methods, these are the steps that work best for me:

1. Prepare using a ceremony that you create with practices from this book to create sacred space.

2. Make music: drum, rattle or use a recording to help shift yourself into a trance state. If you are drumming or rattling on your own, use a repetitive beat at the rate of approximately four beats per second. If you are learning to drum or rattle for yourself, it can be helpful to use a recording at first to help you focus on your journey. As you progress with your own drumming and rattling, you can start playing with the recording and stop when it becomes distracting. When ending a shamanic journey, drum faster and more loudly at the end to help bring yourself completely back into your body and

close the journey. Do not listen to shamanic drumming recordings while driving or doing anything else that requires focus, as your mind may shift whether you intend it to or not.

3. Begin the journey: there are many ways to do this. I am sharing one here that I learned from Norma Nakai Burton, creator of the Journey to Completion shadow integration process. To begin your journey, choose a place that is special to you in ordinary reality and that you know very well. As the drumming for the journey begins, imagine that there is someone with you in this place that will receive you when you return from your journey. Then, find somewhere to begin digging a tunnel to the underworld. Focus on the digging with care and attention. If this digging turns into something else, or calls you to another place, follow that invitation. When you come out of the tunnel, notice where you are and ask a spirit helper to meet you to guide you on your journey. I vet my guides carefully if they are new and I don't have a prior relationship with them. You can ask multiple times if they are a helping spirit for you. Look for four signs from the guide to show you that they are a true spirit helper, such as seeing them from four different angles. Once you are in and have made contact with your spirit helper(s), follow the flow of the journey. If you find yourself thinking or feeling distracted, focus on the sound of the drum to gently bring you back to your journey.

4. Return! When you come back, trace your steps all the way back through your journey. This will help to imprint the journey onto emerging neural pathways and also guarantee that you return completely to your body. I spend at least five minutes making sure that I have completely re-entered my body, breathing into my body from my toes to my head, feeling from the top of my head down through my spine as I anchor myself firmly on the floor or the ground. Take time to reflect on your journey by writing it down or

sharing it with others if you are in a group. This is an important step to help you integrate the journey.

5. Ground: At first, you may feel that you are a bit between two worlds when you start to journey more regularly. You may begin to feel or hear guides when in "normal" consciousness. Over time, your capacity for experiencing these perceptual shifts will grow. If this is disconcerting for you, set the intention to not feel or hear guides or energetic reality outside of journeys. You are in charge of your experience. Set the boundaries and parameters that are comfortable for you. Even though I have had things happen in journeys that felt very uncomfortable and even painful — at one point my heart was removed, and a new one implanted with fire — I always know that I have a choice to stop any interaction or leave the journey at any time.

Ask for Help from Your Spirit Guides

Learn and remember to ask for help early and often. Leave yourself reminders; ask again and again. Asking for help from spirit helpers through each day offers so much guidance and support. It's hard to express how much we need this, and how much our spirit helpers want to give us help. They honor our agency and will not interfere with our life path without our permission. *Ask for help, ask for help, ask for help.* It will always be there, in small or large ways.

The helping spirits of the Earth are all around us now, longing to help us move from this place of incredible pain and damage to the Earth into a new consciousness of care and connection. In this time of unprecedented challenges, the spirit helpers are filled with joy when we ask for help. I offer a prayer of gratitude to all of the helping spirits of the Earth for guiding us home, for showing us the way, for being our ancestors, our predecessors and our spirit families.

Conclusion: Re-Visioning the World One Dream at a Time

Knowing our remorse, pain, anger and grief in the face of the devastation of our Earth home and family is an important step to waking up our senses. We cannot move into alignment with Earth and our true selves without feeling vast wellsprings of pain. We can feel so small in the face of time, in the face of history, in the face of the intractable forces of a civilization that perpetuates the seemingly bottomless degradation of life on this planet.

Yet from this pain, we begin to know that we love the Earth. We begin to feel our way back home; listening to the song that arises in our hearts as we reconnect with Earth, we find our way back into the folds of life. Often, the song begins as a lament, and that is always there in our times. Yet we can find in our hearts, and through love, stories of joy and wonder, community, care for life and amazing human ingenuity to create healing and change. As we wake up, we find there are others already awake and working toward a new way of living in Western culture seemingly everywhere we turn. From my own studies and teaching of sustainability, I now feel true awe at the numbers of people and communities that are creating new stories in their own lives and for their bioregions, all over the world. There is a vast web of new stories, and dreamers weaving their stories into a healing dream for the Earth.

As children, we touch the Earth with wonder and love. We draw lines in the dirt, our primal creativity feeling the skin of our planet with reverence. The magic of childhood is lost in what Gregory Bateson calls the "yoga of occidental education."[94] Over time, we unconsciously "realize" that our primal love for life is childish and "unreasonable." We grow out of this love and forget our belonging. Now is the time to grow back into our love for our planetary home.

In the face of hopelessness and helplessness, we fall back on love: an undervalued resource in our resource-obsessed culture. Love opens our hearts; love finds a way; love leads us back to where we began. Being entranced and filled with the magic of dirt, the light of the sun, the slippery feeling of water falling through our hands, the wind dancing in the trees, sings us into a next step. Remembering who we really are in relation to the rest of life, we forget how to take so much from the Earth. Through our love of the Earth we change so much more than we can imagine is possible.

Loving the Earth, we feel when we step across a line into a new way of being. Though we may not be able or choose to change in that moment, we begin to know where the lines are. We begin to grow into an ethic of care. In circles with others, speaking of nature with reverence, honoring the Earth, we come to grow Earth-honoring communities with new beliefs, new ways of being and knowing each other and new stories.

We Are the Storytellers

We co-create the story of our individual and collective lives one moment, one thought, one engagement with life at a time. Each moment we decide how we will engage with the world, and these decisions add up over time to merge into the larger collection of the story of our species and, because of the profound impact that we are able to exert on the Earth at this time, the story of our planet. This does not mean that we control the world. Instead, we acknowledge our profound power to choose how we engage with the world. To become fully mature humans is to acknowledge that we are creating every moment. It requires seeing and accepting the mantle of responsibility of our impact not only in what we do every day, but also in what we choose to think and how we choose to feel. This is the initiation into our true nature; we are the storytellers, the story-keepers, the ones who vision with symbols and images.

It can be very overwhelming for those of us recovering from mechanistic, objective reality to feel so responsible. We didn't create this giant "machine" of reality. What can we possibly do to change it? Asking these questions, we call out with hopelessness, thrash in anger, cry for guidance. What we can do is allow ourselves to become fully human within the web of a relational story of the universe. While it is true that we are never free from responsibility, we are able to rest in the creation once we turn our lives back into the stories of sacred and joyful relationship with all of life that they are meant to be. Conversely, it is by accepting the truth and responsibility of our "story-creating" nature, and finding our way back to life, that we are finally free.

This chapter helps readers create and share the stories about their Earth Spirit Dreaming visions of healing for the planet. It guides readers through the process of reframing their own sense of meaning and purpose as they integrate the new sensitivities and abilities that they have developed. The primary goal of this chapter is to help readers bring their new abilities and vision into the world.

Changing Our Stories

I grew up with an abusive mother. From many years of struggle, I now know what the pain of not being truly mothered gave me: a profound ability to connect with the Earth. My wound is now my gift. As we tell our stories again and again, we are sifting and shifting; we are creating. We can create new realities, and a new world, by re-visioning our stories, just as I've worked over decades to re-vision mine. Often, this requires gratitude and forgiveness in the face of trauma, betrayal and loss. Our experiences on this plane, in this body, are often bumpy and painful; being in our bodies on Earth is often strange and isolating. However, from a spiritual perspective, without denying our true and painful feelings (I've had 25 years of therapy to process and grow from my childhood!), over time we can find the growth and spiritual silver lining. I know this can sound Pollyanna-ish, and the skepticism of our world often berates this view. But spiritually, shifting in these ways is essential to raising our vibrations and dreaming a new dream for our lives and for the Earth. We can only find light with light. Not by pushing away darkness and pain, but by bringing it with us to a new story in a transmuted form. The energy of my pain has transmuted through my own process of healing into energy that can be shared with the world through my work as a healer and teacher. In this way, we can all "compost" the pain of our lives and the world to grow and create new visions.

It's taken me many years to transform my personal stories. My body remembers pain quite well, and will remind me of hurts, slights and real wrongs done to me through memory triggers that can rapidly awaken paths in my brain and body from the times when these events were occurring. Because of this, it has taken a lot of conscious shifting of my stories over long periods to create new body memories and emotional states.

I know as an energy worker that things can shift in our energy bodies very quickly, while it may take time for the grooves of our physical bodies to adjust to the new reality. This is the same with changing our stories. Because our bodies can have entrenched pathways of memories, it takes mindfulness to catch ourselves when we fall into the ruts of our past stories, and when we are creating future stories through stress, fear and longing. Vibrational work helps us shift our bodies into new modes of experience. Connecting with Earth and Spirit on a regular basis provides a platform for new ways of experience that can gradually replace old ways of being and remembering ourselves and the world. This is a long process that requires commitment: it is the work of a lifetime. Still, regular practice can be short and built into the cracks. Below is a simple method I use to change my stories:

1. I set the intention to notice whenever I am running over painful memories. What are the triggers? What are the body memories? Places, seasons, certain times of the year can trigger old stories. First, just notice. This requires sitting with discomfort. Often, when we start to become aware of these painful stories we are annoyed with how often they pull us in, and we want them, and their pain, to GO AWAY NOW! Loving kindness, gentleness and patience are required while building awareness. And returning to awareness is an ongoing life

practice. If I am tired, overwhelmed, sick, stressed, if it's cloudy, if I've had too much coffee or unhealthy food: bam! My mind can return to the old stories.

2. Develop a reliable image that helps you shift the story. While this seems simple, it can take profound contemplation to find ways to feel love in relation to very difficult or painful stories. Some stories seem impossible to hold with love: the Holocaust, slavery, decimation of the environment, killing of indigenous people ... these are examples of times when I turn to spirit helpers to help me see in new ways and with new images. We cannot transmute painful personal or global stories on our own. Sometimes, all we can do is hold them in light from our hearts, and ask the Great Spirit of the Universe and our spirit helpers to guide us toward new ways of being with these stories.

3. Attempt to catch your mind and body running over the painful stories and replace it with the new image and accompanying emotional signature. This can be a split-second thing to do, and will probably need to be done over and over again. Just catching ourselves and shifting is huge and profound work.

4. As often as you can, take time to immerse yourself in the visualization of the new story, so that when you are going about your daily routine and have to make a shift, the feeling and images are more readily available to you.

Begin with Love

We create healing stories when we start with love. Large portions of Western thought and beliefs are now reintegrating the ancient truth that everything is connected. In the pageant of the cosmos, with us in everything, and everything in us, we are never alone. We no longer have to figure things out alone, or just with other humans. In fact, this is how we got in this mess to begin with. Instead, we start with active love and let the new dreams and visions for our lives arise within the matrix of this connection. It is through love that we find the imprint of the underlying energetic fabric of life, allow this to permeate us and vision from this expanded and amplified understanding far beyond our human limitations.

So now, we come to the final practice of the book; the most important practice; a place to always start and finish. If we do only one practice each day, and this is always mine, we learn to love the Earth and dream our lives from this place. It is a practice that I have learned by loving and dreaming with the Earth that always shepherds me out of the maze of separation into the gossamer labyrinth of connection, where finding my way becomes a magical, spiritual journey of becoming in community. Our rational minds crave complexity of ideas while paradoxically minimizing the complexity of life, because the truth of how much we don't know can be frightening. So, we too often find ourselves in a constricting cave of confusion instead of on a sometimes wild path of creation. As I've written before in this book, and truly and deeply believe, while we can never understand the Divine Mystery of life, we can always relate. It is our hearts that take us there, and often through means that seem too simple to be able to make true changes. This is the gift and miracle of love; so challenging to get ourselves there yet so simple once we are there. We can always touch the Earth; that is something to always go back to and begin with.

EXERCISE: Loving the Earth
Purpose

> In Western culture, we are energetically oriented toward taking from the Earth. Just as we pull energy into ourselves, as discussed in earlier chapters, so we are in an unconscious habit of pulling energy from the Earth. We take from the Earth in every moment in our lives. As a culture, Westerners harvest the lifeblood of the earth and her family to feed our lives, often mindlessly, or when we become mindful, in confusion of why it is so hard to stop. One place to begin is by shifting our conscious orientation of our energy. We are

always sending or receiving, as I share in Chapter Ten, and this is never more true than in how we orient ourselves energetically to the Earth.

We can become attentive to the pull of our consciousness on the Earth by intentionally loving the Earth every day. There are many ways to do this; I've described a couple of them here. As many of the practices in this book teach, we begin by using our imagination. Just like any loving relationship, our understanding and love of the Earth grows over time — we begin to find our own dance with the Earth through active love; the Earth will begin to express herself to you, to reach out to and into you and to gradually show more of herself through contact and deepening intimacy.

Description

Intentionally feel love for the Earth. If this feels strange at first, imagine a person or companion animal who you love, then transfer this feeling to the Earth. One way that I love the Earth, and encourage others to do so, is to imagine that I am sending love through my feet to the Earth, either through an intentional walking meditation or as I'm walking throughout the day. I imagine that I am breathing in divine light and love and breathing it out through the bottom of my feet to the Earth. It is in walking that we are most often touching Earth. Making this a conscious practice of giving energy means it becomes a walking mantra of love. When the weather permits, I put my bare feet on the ground to love the Earth through my feet. The more contact the better.

Another way to love the Earth is to imagine that you are holding the Earth like a baby in your arms. Loving and hugging the Earth. Just like for spirit helpers, the orientation toward love and gratitude helps us to hear the voice of the Earth. The heaviness of many human thought forms and states closes the channels of communication with Earth, her beings, spirits, elemental energies and body memories. The shift that comes to us through love opens channels for her to communicate her dreams to us. The Earth is joyful to have us return to her. Just as an infected limb would distract and hurt, so our species being unwell puts the entire organism of the planet into distress. Feeling us come back into alignment relieves stress and the pull of the energy that we take in our disorientation. As we come into alignment with the dream of the Earth, our own lives feel more fulfilling and life giving. We can leave offerings and loving art for the Earth. We can thank the Earth with every moment of what we do. The Earth and all of nature love to hear songs, to have us dance in joy with and about the creation, to drum with the heartbeat of the Earth, honoring her.

My personal and favorite practice is to lay hands on the Earth, to be an energy healer for the Earth. As I have come to feel the memories of this life and others backward and forward through time with my clients, I've realized that through the energy healing for the Earth I now move into a knowing of the body memories of the Earth, the memories held in the Earth's body backward and forward through time. The first time I felt this, it was so big that I panicked and stopped my practice for quite a while. It would be a book in itself to try to describe this experience. Suffice to say that I can never understand, or even orient my mind, in these moments. It is a falling-into, a merging that obliterates my senses with smells, sights, emotions, images, spirits, happenings past and future. I know that this feeling with and knowing the Earth on this level cannot be done alone. While I still do this practice on my own, I also do it every time I am in a ceremonial group, usually keeping it to myself, to ground the circle and to honor the memories, the pains, the joys, the past and future stories of the Earth.

Following Love – Re-Visioning Earth

Re-visioning Earth, re-dreaming the stories of our lives, is the journey of a lifetime; it is the journey and the task of OUR lifetime as a species. We are in grave peril as a species if we do not embrace, reclaim and enact these ancestral ways of being. We must create a new world! Many already are, and as you immerse yourself in this Great Work (Berry), or Great Turning (Macy) — and you already have — you will find a great sweep of changes, a vast network of light beings shifting the consciousness on the planet. This is challenging work; the single most important thing we can do as citizens of the Earth, and as spirits committed to the karmic unfolding of the planetary dream.

Following love means to listen to our bodies, to trust our feelings, and to do this in community that is aligned with healing and reverence for life. Dreaming a new dream, owning our responsibility to tell life-giving, life-honoring stories, requires actively replanting ourselves in our natural environment. Out of the "pot" of industrial indoor culture, to outdoor living, fully rooted in the Earth, open to the sun and the many beings that sing to us from all around the living universe. In order to take part as healing dreamers we must give ourselves what we need to be truly, healthy humans. A plant in a dark room, a pot that is too small, too wet, too dry, cannot grow into the best version of itself. So, too, we need to "replant" ourselves into the Earth sensitivities that are our evolutionary inheritance. With the right environment of intentionally relating to life with love, our stories naturally begin to reflect a healing vision. Our job is to connect and honor life; we are story-makers and the stories will begin to shift on their own. When the new stories begin to grow we feed them and water them by bringing them into the light of community. Reflecting back to others. Yes, I hear you, I see you. You are not crazy. There is love, and joy, and truth to be found with our feet planted firmly on the Earth in circles of song and sharing.

The practices in this book, and all Earth-healing practices, required to change the world are hard and require fortitude and unprecedented mindfulness. Along with knowing that everything is connected, the most important concept in this book is that as we heal our own lives, we heal the world. Re-visioning for ourselves makes us warriors of light for re-visioning the world. We all realign together as we are one, expressions of the divine light of life. We can consciously turn these skills of re-visioning, changing our story, toward changing the direction, vibrations and story of the world. Once we have developed the skills inherent in our human history — Earth-connecting, Spirit-connecting — we can begin to dream a new dream from the place of connection and love and intention for healing.

We have all that we need to return to the core of our genetic gateway to the stories and memories of the Earth, the true magic on this planet.

Rhythms and cycles govern every aspect of our lives and reconnecting with these rhythms is the way back to our true nature. The sun rises and sets, we rise and sleep. We are both alive and we die, in cycles of soul, of spirit, of body. We breathe with the trees, we live through the seasons of years, generations and geological time.

List of Exercises

Earth-Connecting Practices

Unstructured Time and Musing	68
Cultivating Ecological Consciousness	69
Small Moments with Nature	74
Spending Time Outdoors Each Day	75
Walking Barefoot on the Ground	76
A Grounding Meditation	77
Sitting or Lying on the Earth	78
Lying on the Earth, by Thich Nhat Hanh	79
Sitting or Lying Down with Rocks	80
Creating a Set of Sacred Stones	81
Find and Return to a Special Natural Place	85
Connecting with Nature Beings in Your Sacred Place	88
The Ecophenomenology of Rocks	89
Simple Sacred Nature Art	94
Working with Ancient Symbols	95
Spiral Meditation	97
Nature Collage	99
Plants and Nature Art	100

Spirit-Connecting Practices

Creating Sacred Space	121
Grounding to the Earth	123
Setting Clear Intentions	124
Immersion with the Four Directions	128
Clearing Sacred Space	129
Opening Your Heart	131
Waking Up Your Energy Body: Creating Your Ball of Light	132

Calling Your Spirit Back to You 134
Karmic Eddy Mandala Drawing 138
Karmic Eddy Clearing 140

Dream-Connecting Practices

Gather Your Medicine 167
Listening to Your Sacred Stones 169
Visioning Collage Mandala 173
Circling Mandala Meditation 174
Inviting Spirit Symbols with Mandalas 177
Working with Visioning Rocks 178
Creating Your Sacred Space in Shamanic Reality 190
Visioning with Nature Beings – Becoming Fully Human 193
Creating Rituals for Trance States 195
Shamanic Journeying 197
Loving the Earth 206

Reference Notes

1. Annie Leonard, "Moving from Individual to Societal Change," *State of the World: Is Sustainability Still Possible?* (Washington, DC: Worldwatch Institute, 2013).
2. Aldo Leopold, "The Land Ethic," *A Sand County Almanac* (Oxford: Oxford University Press, 1949/1987).
3. See Owen Barfield, *Saving the Appearances: A Study in Idolatry* (Middletown, CT: Wesleyan University Press, 1988), for a detailed discussion of the suppression of "primitive" levels of awareness in Western culture.
4. Thomas Berry, *The Dream of the Earth* (Berkeley, CA: Counterpoint; reprint edition, 2015), 211-12.
5. Berry, *The Dream of the Earth*, 211-12.
6. "One Planet Living," from Global Footprint Network, reprinted in *State of the World: Is Sustainability Still Possible?*, Worldwatch Institute, 2013, (Moore, Rees 2013: 41).
7. Dolores LaChapelle, "Ritual is Essential," *Art and Ceremony in Sustainable Culture*, Spring, 1984, Context Institute.
8. LaChapelle, *"Ritual is Essential."*
9. Barfield, *Saving the Appearances.*
10. Michael J. Cohen, *Reconnecting With Nature* (Apple Valley, MN: Ecopress, an imprint of Finney Company; third edition, 2007), 33.
11. James Lovelock, *Gaia: A New Look at Life on Earth* (Oxford: Oxford University Press, 1995).
12. Paul Hawken, *Blessed Unrest: How the Largest Social Movement in History Is Restoring Grace, Justice, and Beauty to the World* (New York: Viking, 2007).
13. Hawken, *Blessed Unrest*, 84-85.
14. Thanks to my friend Robert Toth for deepening my understanding of the idea of "holonic consciousness" as an effective means of differentiating from "anthropocentric consciousness."
15. Thomas Berry, *The Great Work* (Danvers, MA: Broadway Books; reprint edition, 2000), 82.
16. Berry, *The Dream of the Earth.*
17. Berry, *The Dream of the Earth.*

18. Ralph Waldo Emerson, *Nature* (Boston and Cambridge: James Munroe and Company, 1836/1949).
19. This table is derived in part by reference to David Skrbina's dissertation, "Participation, Organization, and Mind: Toward a Participatory Worldview" (2001), 11–15.
20. Tony Moodie, "Re-evaluating the idea of indigenous knowledge: Implications of anti-dualism in African philosophy and theology." Paper presented at the annual conference of the African Studies Association of Australia and the Pacific (AFSAAP), University of Western Australia, November 26–28, 2004.
21. Arne Naess, in Rothenberg, David, ed., *Is It Painful to Think? Conversations with Arne Naess* (Minneapolis, MN: University of Minnesota Press, 1993).
22. Joanna Macy, *World as Lover, World as Self* (Berkeley, CA: Parallax Press, 1991).
23. Macy, *World as Lover, World as Self*, 187.
24. Joanna Macy, with Molly Young Brown, *Coming Back to Life: The Updated Guide to the Work That Reconnects* (Gabriola Island, BC: New Society Publishers, Limited, 2014).
25. Macy, *Coming Back to Life,* 46.
26. Macy, *Coming Back to Life,* 47.
27. Macy, *Coming Back to Life,* 47.
28. From Paul Hawken's website, blessedunrest.com.
29. Susan Griffin, *Woman and Nature: The Roaring Inside Her* (Berkeley, CA: Counterpoint Press, 2016).
30. Griffin, *Woman and Nature*.
31. Ralph Metzner, *Green Psychology: Transforming Our Relationship to the Earth* (Rochester, VT: Park Street Press, 1999), 86–87.
32. Metzner, *Green Psychology,* 85.
33. Paul Shepard, *Nature and Madness* (Athens, GA: University of Georgia Press, 2011).
34. Metzner, *Green Psychology,* 86–87.
35. Alexander von Humboldt is considered the father of the field of ecology, in that he was the first known Western thinker to study relationships between organisms and their environment. Humboldt's discipline was named *oecologie*, or ecology, by Ernst Haeckel in 1866, in his *General Morphology of Organisms (Morphologie der Organismen)*. Learn more in Andrea Wulf, *The Invention of Nature: Alexander von Humboldt's New World*, Random House, 2016.
36. Theodore Roszak, *The Voice of the Earth: An Exploration of Ecopsychology* (Grand Rapids, MI: Phanes, 2001).

37. Betty Roszak, "Rescue and Restore," from Roszak, *The Voice of the Earth*, dedication.
38. Roszak, "Rescue and Restore."
39. Leopold, "The Land Ethic."
40. This idea is informed by and expands the concept of the ecological self, originated by Arne Naess in his book *The Ecology of Wisdom* (Berkeley, CA: Counterpoint Press, 2010).
41. Leopold, "The Land Ethic."
42. Karen Warren, "The power and the promise of ecofeminism, revisited," in Michael Zimmerman, ed., *Environmental Philosophy: From Animal Rights to Radical Ecology* (Upper Saddle River, NJ: Pearson/Prentice Hall, 2005).
43. Henryk Skolimowski, *The Participatory Mind: A New Theory of Knowledge and of the Universe* (New York: Penguin Books; first edition, 1995).
44. These passages are adapted from my dissertation, "From Emerson to Macy: The Evolution of a Participatory Worldview," 2011, San Francisco, CA: California Institute of Integral Studies.
45. Cohen, *Reconnecting With Nature*, 33.
46. Cohen, *Reconnecting With Nature*, 33.
47. For another exercise to deepen this experience of connectedness, see my article entitled "The Self System Drawing: Teaching a Sustainable Worldview through Creativity," in *The Journal of Sustainability Education*, 2014.
48. Qing Li, a professor at Nippon Medical School in Tokyo, along with his research partners, conducted studies that measured cellular activity of the immune system before and after a visit to a forest. See his article, "Effect of phytoncide from trees on human natural killer cell function," *Int J Immunopathol Pharmacol*. 2009 Oct–Dec; 22 (4): 951–9.
49. Nachman of Bratzlav, translation by Shamai Kanter, *Kol Haneshamah, Shabbat Vehagim* (Wyncote, PA: The Reconstructionist Press, 1994).
50. Clinton Ober, et al. *Earthing: The Most Important Health Discovery Ever!* (Laguna Beach, CA: Basic Health Publications, Incorporated, 2014).
51. Thich Nhat Hanh, "I Want to Be Grounded" (*Shambhala Sun*, July 2012).
52. Nhat Hanh, "I Want to Be Grounded."
53. Adapted from Rhea Loader, *Dreamstones: Magic from the Living Earth* (London: Prism Press, 1991).
54. William Cahalan, "Ecological Groundedness in Gestalt Therapy," from *Ecopsychology: Restoring the Earth, Healing the Mind*, ed. Theodore Roszak, Mary E. Gomes and Allen D. Kanner (San Francisco, CA: Sierra Club Books, 1995), 216–23.
55. Cahalan, "Ecological Groundedness in Gestalt Therapy," 216–23.
56. Cohen, *Reconnecting with Nature*, 23.

57. Rudolf Steiner, *How to Know Higher Worlds: A Modern Path of Initiation* (Great Barrington, MA: Anthroposophic Press, 2014).
58. These questions are derived in part from David Wood, "What is Ecophenomenology?," *Research in Phenomenology*, 31 (1):78–95 (2001).
59. Berry, *Dream of the Earth*, 211.
60. Macy, *Coming Back to Life*.
61. Michael G. Reccia, *The Joseph Communications: Revelation. Who You Are; Why You're Here* (N.p.: eBookit.com, 2012).
62. Thanks to Carole Wallencheck for pointing out that the origin of weird is wyrd, meaning destiny.
63. Berry, *The Great Work*.
64. Reccia, *The Joseph Communications: Revelation*.
65. Michael Laitman, *A Glimpse of Light: The Basics of the Wisdom of Kabbalah* (Brooklyn, NY: Laitman Kabbalah Publishers, 2013).
66. Laitman, *A Glimpse of Light*, 123.
67. Llyn Roberts and Robert Levy, *Shamanic Reiki: Expanded Ways of Working with Universal Life Force Energy* (Alresford, UK: Moon Books, 2007).
68. Reccia, *The Joseph Communications: Revelation*.
69. Ervin Laszlo, *The Systems View of the World: A Holistic Vision for Our Time* (New York: Hampton Press, 1996).
70. Laszlo, *The Systems View of the World*, 82.
71. Macy, *Coming Back to Life*, 42.
72. Jerrold J. Abrams, "Peirce, Kant, and Apel on transcendental semiotics: The unity of apperception and the deduction of the categories of signs," *Transactions of the Charles S. Peirce Society*, 2004, 40 (4): 627–77.
73. Cynthia Overweg, "Hildegard of Bingen: The Nun Who Loved the Earth" (Quest 105:3 Summer 2017), 21–25.
74. David Bohm, in Ken Wilber, ed., *The Holographic Paradigm and Other Paradoxes* (Boston, MA: Shambhala Publications, 1982).
75. Bohm, in Wilber, *The Holographic Paradigm and Other Paradoxes*, 62.
76. Bohm, in Wilber, *The Holographic Paradigm and Other Paradoxes*, 40–41.
77. Amit Goswami, *The Visionary Window: A Quantum Physicist's Guide to Enlightenment* (Wheaton, IL: Quest Books, 2012).
78. Goswami, *The Visionary Window*, 110.
79. Goswami, *The Visionary Window*, 137.
80. Willard van Orman Quine, *Ontological Relativity and Other Essays* (New York: Columbia University Press, 1969).
81. Carl G. Jung, *The Red Book: Liber Novus* (New York: W. W. Norton & Company; first edition, 19 October, 2009).
82. Jung, *The Red Book: Liber Novus*.

83. Jung, "Mysterium. Encounter," HI v(v), *The Red Book: Liber Novus.*
84. Sandra Ingerman, "Medicine for the Earth." In Llewellyn Vaughan-Lee, ed., *Spiritual Ecology: The Cry of the Earth* (Point Reyes Station, CA: Golden Sufi Center, 2016).
85. Ingerman, "Medicine for the Earth," 232.
86. Christina Pratt, *An Encyclopedia of Shamanism* (Buffalo, NY: Rosen Publishing Group; first edition, 1 June, 2007).
87. Pratt, *An Encyclopedia of Shamanism,* xliii.
88. There are many places to find information on the vast movement of Earth spirituality and action that is arising in Western religions. Two great places to start are the book *This Sacred Earth: Religion, Nature, Environment,* edited by Roger Gottlieb (New York: Routledge, 2004) and the film *Renewal* (http://www.renewalproject.net/film). There are religious groups in almost every region, and many countries, that are reorienting their understanding, stewardship, and liturgy toward honoring and caring for the Earth. Look in your own area to find these activists to learn more.
89. Bill Pfeiffer, *Wild Earth, Wild Soul: A Manual for an Ecstatic Culture* (Alresford, UK: Moon Books, 2013), 18.
90. Gottlieb, *This Sacred Earth.*
91. Adapted from *Dreamstones: Magic from the Living Earth* (London: Prism Press: 1990), 56.
92. Ronald Reminick, et al. *Healing Across Cultures & The Good Life: An Approach to Holistic Health* (Farmington Hills, MI: Cengage Learning, 2010), 51.
93. The idea of resting in our "true self" in shamanic reality is given to me by my friend and shamanic mentor, Damaris Chrystal.
94. Gregory Bateson, *Steps to an Ecology of Mind* (Chicago, IL: University of Chicago Press, 2000).

Selected Reading

Abrams, Jerrold J. "Peirce, Kant, and Apel on transcendental semiotics: The unity of apperception and the deduction of the categories of signs." *Transactions of the Charles S. Peirce Society* 40 (4): 627–77.

Barfield, Owen. *Saving the Appearances: A Study in Idolatry*. Middletown, CT: Wesleyan University Press, 1988.

Bateson, Gregory. *Steps to an Ecology of Mind*. Chicago, IL: University of Chicago Press, 2000.

Berry, Thomas. *The Dream of the Earth*. Berkeley, CA: Counterpoint Press, 2015.

———. *The Great Work: Our Way into the Future*. Danvers, MA: Broadway Books; reprint edition, 2000.

Cahalan, William. "Ecological Groundedness in Gestalt Therapy," from *Ecopsychology: Restoring the Earth, Healing the Mind*, ed. Theodore Roszak, Mary E. Gomes, and Allen D. Kanner. San Francisco, CA: Sierra Club Books, 1995.

Cohen, Michael J. *Reconnecting with Nature*. Apple Valley, MN: Ecopress, an imprint of Finney Company; third edition, 2007.

Emerson, Ralph Waldo. *Nature*. Boston and Cambridge: James Munroe and Company, 1836/1949.

Goswami, Amit. *The Visionary Window: A Quantum Physicist's Guide to Enlightenment*. Wheaton, IL: Quest Books, 2012.

Gottlieb, Roger S., ed. *This Sacred Earth: Religion, Nature, Environment*. New York: Routledge, 2004.

Griffin, Susan. *Woman and Nature: The Roaring Inside Her*. Berkeley, CA: Counterpoint Press, 2016.

Hanh, Thich Nhat. "I Want to Be Grounded." *Shambhala Sun*, July 2012.

Hawken, Paul. *Blessed Unrest: How the Largest Social Movement in History is Restoring Grace, Justice, and Beauty to the World*. New York: Viking, 2007.

Ingerman, Sandra. "Medicine for the Earth." In Llewellyn Vaughan Lee, ed. *Spiritual Ecology: The Cry of the Earth*. Point Reyes Station, CA: Golden Sufi Center, 2016.

Jung, C. G. *The Red Book: Liber Novus*. New York: W. W. Norton & Company; first edition, 19 October 2009.

Kol Haneshama: Shabbat Vehagim. Wyncote, PA: The Reconstructionist Press, 1994.

Laitman, Michael. *A Glimpse of Light: The Basics of the Wisdom of Kabbalah*. Brooklyn, NY: Laitman Kabbalah Publishers, 2013.

Laszlo, Ervin. *The Systems View of the World: A Holistic Vision for Our Time*. New York: Hampton Press, 1996.

Leonard, Annie. "Moving from Individual Change to Societal Change." In *State of the World: Is Sustainability Still Possible?* Washington, DC: Worldwatch Institute, 2013.

Leopold, Aldo, and Michael Sewell. *A Sand County Almanac*. Oxford: Oxford University Press, 2001.

Li, Qing. "Effect of phytoncide from trees on human natural killer cell function," *Int J Immunopathol Pharmacol*. 2009 Oct–Dec;22(4):951-9.

Loader, Rhea. *Dreamstones: Magic from the Living Earth*. London: Prism Press, 1990.

Lovelock, James. *Gaia: A New Look at Life on Earth*. Oxford: Oxford University Press, 1995.

Macy, Joanna. *World as Lover, World as Self: Courage for Global Justice and Ecological Renewal*. Berkeley, CA: Parallax Press, 2007.

Macy, Joanna, and Molly Young Brown. *Coming Back to Life: The Updated Guide to the Work That Reconnects*. Gabriola Island, BC: New Society Publishers, 2014.

Meacham, Elizabeth. "From Emerson to Macy: The Evolution of a Participatory Worldview," a dissertation at the California Institute of Integral Studies, 2011.

———. "The Self System Drawing: Teaching a Sustainable Worldview through Creativity." In *The Journal of Sustainability Education*, 2014.

Metzner, Ralph. *Green Psychology: Transforming Our Relationship to the Earth*. Rochester, VT: Park Street Press, 1999.

Moodie, Tony. "Re-evaluating the idea of indigenous knowledge: Implications of anti-dualism in African philosophy and theology." Paper presented at the annual conference of the African Studies Association of Australia and the Pacific (AFSAAP), University of Western Australia, 26–28 November, 2004.

Ober, Clinton, Stephen T. Sinatra, and Martin Zucker. *Earthing: The Most Important Health Discovery Ever!* Laguna Beach, CA: Basic Health Publications, 2014.

Overweg, Cynthia. "Hildegard of Bingen: The Nun Who Loved the Earth." *Quest* 105:3 Summer 2017.

Pfeiffer, Bill. *Wild Earth, Wild Soul: A Manual for an Ecstatic Culture*. Alresford, UK: Moon Books, 2013.

Pratt, Christina. *An Encyclopedia of Shamanism*. Buffalo, NY: Rosen Publishing Group, 2007.

Quine, Willard Van Orman. *Ontological Relativity and Other Essays*. New York: Columbia University Press, 1969.

Reccia, Michael G. *The Joseph Communications: Revelation. Who You Are; Why You're Here*. N.p.: eBookit.com, 2012.

Reminick, Ronald, Todd Pesek, and Murali Nair. *Healing Across Cultures & The Good Life: An Approach to Holistic Health*. Farmington Hills, MI: Cengage Learning, 2010.

Roberts, Llyn, and Robert Levy. *Shamanic Reiki: Expanded Ways of Working with Universal Life Force Energy*. Alresford, UK: Moon Books, 2007.

Roszak, Theodore. *The Voice of the Earth: An Exploration of Ecopsychology*. Grand Rapids, MI: Phanes, 2001.

Rothenberg, David. *Is It Painful to Think? Conversations with Arne Naess*. Minneapolis, MN: University of Minnesota Press, 1993.

Shepard, Paul. *Nature and Madness*. Athens, GA: University of Georgia Press, 2011.

Skolimowski, Henryk. *The Participatory Mind: A New Theory of Knowledge and of the Universe*. New York: Arkana/Penguin Books, 1994.

Skrbina, David. "Participation, Organization, and Mind: Toward a participatory worldview." Bath, U.K: Center for Action Research in Professional Practice, University of Bath, 2001.

Steiner, Rudolph. *How to Know Higher Worlds*. Great Barrington, MA: Anthroposophic Press, 1994.

Wilbur, Ken, ed. *The Holographic Paradigm and Other Paradoxes*. Boston, MA: Shambhala Publications, 1982.

Wood, David. "What Is Ecophenomenology?" *Research in Phenomenology*, 31 (1):78—95 (2001).

Wulf, Andrea. *The Invention of Nature: Alexander von Humboldt's New World*. New York: Random House, 2016.

Zimmerman, Michael, ed. *Environmental Philosophy: From Animal Rights to Radical Ecology*. Upper Saddle River, NJ: Pearson/Prentice Hall, 2005.

Acknowledgments

First and foremost, I thank the Great Spirit of the Universe, Divine Creator, Holy Spirit, Shekhinah, God, the Source of all Love, for my life and all that is good. Thank you to my husband, Mattuck Meacham, for making my dreams possible and for long discussions as we each imagined our books into the world together. Thank you to my children for bringing so much joy to my life and hope for a better world.

A special thank-you to my dear friend and colleague, Nurete Brenner, for helping me honor my earthy-spiritual intelligence, and for years of reflection and feedback on the ideas in this book. Thank you to Bill Pfeiffer, for helping me trust my path and for input on my book proposal and early chapters. Thank you to Christopher Bache for guiding me to Findhorn Press, for his lovely foreword and general support and inspiring conversations about our work.

Thank you to my dad and beloved stepmother, Terry and Nancy Elsberry, for their constant love, encouragement and support for my work; to my sister, Anne Warrington, for always believing in me; to my mother, Jan Sturgis, for birthing me, raising me and teaching me that women can be gifted and powerful spiritual leaders; to my dear friends, Heidi Abrams and Ellen Hoffman, for their patient emotional support through the process of writing this book.

I am grateful to Sabine Weeke, and the team at Findhorn Press, for capturing and expressing the essence of my book with grace and integrity. Sabine's calm and steady hand made the editing process smooth and delightful.

Thank you, also, to my excellent and encouraging editor, Jacqui Lewis, and to Damian Keenen for the beautiful text design and layout. Heartfelt gratitude to Richard Crookes for a stunning and perceptive cover. Also, thank you to Jon Graham, at Inner Traditions, for sticking with this book.

Finally, a special thank-you to Jill Mattuck Tarule, for encouraging me to trust my own ways of knowing and to follow my star. May her memory and life's work continue to be a blessing.

About the Author

Photo by Mattuck Meacham

Elizabeth E. Meacham, Ph.D., is an internationally recognized environmental philosopher and spiritual ecologist. The founder of the Lake Erie Institute for Holistic Environmental Education in Cleveland, Ohio, she is a practicing shamanic ecotherapist and leads trainings and workshops nationally and internationally.

Elizabeth received her PhD in Philosophy, Cosmology, and Consciousness from the California Institute of Integral Studies and publishes in the areas of creativity, contemplative ecology, sustainability, ecopsychology and shamanic practices. She is also a multi-instrumental musician, writes and performs original ecospiritual music, and integrates music into her teaching and workshops. Elizabeth lives in Cleveland, Ohio.

For more information visit: www.elizabethmeacham.com

FINDHORN PRESS

Life-Changing Books

Learn more about us and our books at
www.findhornpress.com

For information on the Findhorn Foundation:
www.findhorn.org